Mental Gymnastics

Mental Gymnastics

Dr. Leonard F. Anglis, DDS

ISBN 978-0-557-46601-6

This book is dedicated to my wife, Nancy. It is through her help and support that I have been able to complete this book. She makes everything bigger, better, and more successful.

Preface

I have been sitting here dreaming about my life as a dentist. Many people may not know this, but from the very beginning of my elementary school years, I had plans to pursue dentistry as a profession. I now have patients come in and tell my staff that they remember me doing a demonstration of toothbrushing in the second grade. All of my science projects were tooth-related. In sixth grade, I remember writing a term paper on teeth. So I am convinced that I was always destined to become a dentist. All my high school and college courses were taken in preparation for dental school and my life as a dentist. Even though thirty years have passed, I recall how proud I was of my accomplishments at my graduation ceremony as though it was yesterday.

This has been thirty years of learning new procedures to add proficiency to what I do in making my patients smile. My world as a dentist has been changing so fast that what I do now in my dental practice was not done when I graduated from dental school thirty years ago. There had to be an openness to change. As fast as my life as a dentist occurred over my thirty years of practice, I will probably see that much change in the next ten years and then again in the next five. No matter what you do, there is going to be a similar change. The average person changes jobs at least seven times in a lifetime. Long gone are the days of starting up with a firm, business, or factory and then retiring from that same concern. There has to be a certain attitude to go along with this change and a certain psychology to allow the body and the mind to accept it. Acceptance is the first step, but more important is how the body and mind adapt to the stress of the changes in our routine.

I remember seeing a chart of life occurrences. Each had a point value attached to it. The more points, the more stress. The purpose of the chart was to show that if a certain point value of stress was accumulated in a year's time, there would be an increased chance of stress-related illness. Some of the top point-getters were marriage, divorce, signing a mortgage, discovering a major illness, and a death in the family. These were followed by an assortment of other events with correspondingly lower values. It is my belief that the lower-valued stresses are now so numerous that the addition process would take us to a dangerous level without our even being aware of it. We need to develop strategies to shield us from this accumulation of negative forces within us.

Change is one thing, but there are also occurrences throughout our lives that we have to deal with that cause stress to the body. These can be good or bad, but these issues need to have a specific way of being dealt with to enable us to move past them and get on to the next process. This book contains my personal discoveries regarding how to deal with the different occurrences of life, to make sense of them and go on in an improved fashion afterward. The people who live the longest are those who find ways to deal with adversity and put a positive spin on it: to always have a positive outlook at life; to always look for the best in every situation, no matter how difficult it looks initially.

In the culture of the United States, there is an internal pressure to succeed at our jobs and to become successful at what we do. In other cultures, the job and the success are not that important. We have to be mindful of this pressure that we put ourselves under. We need to develop strategies to maximize our time, to make our dreams come true. We also need to preserve our time of rest and have memorable times with the ones we love.

The name of this book is *Mental Gymnastics*, in honor of Dr. Harold Wirth. Like me, he was a dentist. He was part of a movement in dentistry around 1930 to find techniques that could satisfy patients' needs—first by saving teeth, but also by restoring them in such a way so that new problems would not occur. Dr. Wirth was a master in finding positive ways of looking at the world, and he energized himself in a unique fashion. Although he was a dentist, and often put in long hours at work, he developed certain techniques to get him up and going and feeling thankful for dentistry. Dr. Wirth titled these methods mental gymnastics.

I hope you take something especially good and useful from our time together in these next few hours. Remember that I am not professing to be an expert in this matter; I am a student of life, like you. Much of my material will have a certain spin because of my profession. If you will look past that fact, I believe that this will be a useful guide for anyone who picks it up. Because our lives have differed, some of the things I am going to discuss may seem very elemental, and you may wonder why I am writing about them. Other recommendations may not make sense because you have not been in that situation yet. Wait a minute or so, and that situation may occur for you, too!

Finally, I have to admit that this is more a collection of others people's ideas and how they have each changed my life for the better. It could be likened to a bouquet of roses. Each rose represents an idea from someone. The only thing I am providing is the ribbon that holds them all together. I have tried to acknowledge my sources when I am sure I am using the exact words of another. I have listened to audiotapes in my car for years. The ideas I have learned have been incorporated with mine so that it is difficult for me to tell one from the other. I know I have extensively studied books, tapes, and lectures from several authors, including Jim Rohn, Brian Tracy, Zig Ziglar, Dan Kennedy, Pastor Joel Osteen, Dr. L. D. Pankey, and Dr. Harold Wirth. I remember I was at a Jim Rohn lecture, and there were five of us at the lunch table critiquing Jim's performance that day. We all had listened to his material so often we knew when he missed a word or his cadence was off. I will confess early that my ideas have certainly been inspired by others, and you may recognize their inspiration throughout this book.

    Wishing you only the best! Len

Contents

The Decompression Chamber

Where do I start on this journey with you? To make sense in my mind, I initially thought I would keep things in a chronological order as they happened to me. But this thought process did not allow for a good flow to the material, so I am going to write about some things as they are in the present. As we move along, I will insert writings I have made throughout my life that seem to fit. I want to be sure you understand that I am not picking out things in a particular order. Life, of course, is not stacked in an ordered sequence. The cards are shuffled, and we deal with things as if one card was turned over, and then the next. It may be that in this game, cards get reshuffled, or the game or the rules change. It is odd that I would start this first chapter talking about a game. As I deal with challenging issues, I think of much of life as a game, and I try to gain control of the game and find some way to push it in my favor.

Since sometimes the bad things that happen in our lives seem to be the things that we dwell on, and can be a definite drain on our energy and our health, I figured I would spend this first chapter dealing with what I personally do to get past the "stuff" that happens.

One of the symptoms of having a negative change in our lives is that we might not be sleeping as we should. You might not be able to get to sleep, or after you have been asleep for awhile, you wake up and are not able to get back to sleep. This has been a particularly difficult problem for me in the past. Whenever I get to thinking too much, it's hard to shut down and get to sleep. I can definitely tell you not to rely on sleeping pills, alcohol, or both. No matter how nonaddicting a sleeping medication is advertised to be, it can create a psychological dependency that is far stronger than any chemical dependency. Alcohol can induce sleep, but it also disrupts the sleep rhythms so that the sleep is not natural, and it is not restful. Alcohol used in this fashion can very easily lead to the surfacing of alcoholism. If the problems are severe enough, the amount of medication to induce sleep may be high enough that the medication can start affecting you in other ways, possibly making you more prone to depression. If the doctor gives you a medication to help with sleep for a few days to get you through a particularly bad time, take it—but be sure to start finding your own solution so you can limit and eliminate the medication as soon as possible.

What can you do when you are having trouble sleeping? First, there are times when a problem is out of control. It seems like it is a swirling mass, and it tends to spin faster, faster, and faster … and lack of sleep makes it spin almost like a whirlpool. It is hard to break the cycle until more information is obtained. Sometimes making a phone call is all we need to do to get more information. Sometimes we can't get the information right away.

The notice that the IRS is going to investigate the books of your business provides no information until you have your first meeting. Until then, how do you gain some sense of control of the situation? Well, you can't—directly. You have to look at other aspects of your life and start to get control of them. It does not have to be anything sophisticated. Even the small task of organizing your closet can help. Going through your drawers and throwing out what is not necessary and organizing the drawer in a small way will make you feel better. Organization around the house or the office will give you a sense of accomplishment and order that will reduce the out-of-control feeling caused by your bigger problem. These activities are perfect for the times when you can't sleep, since something productive will be done, it will occupy your mind, and it will not give you anything to dwell upon afterwards. Sometimes you will escape your problem long enough that you can get a few hours of needed sleep.

You can also get your mind away from your problem by listening to recorded messages. These can be of a motivational, spiritual, or business nature. For me, the best tapes to listen to are motivational or spiritual. The messages, if crafted correctly, will help you find peace of mind and also a positive way to look at what is going on around you. If you pay attention, your mind will be taken somewhere else. No matter what is happening around you, put in a tape reminding you that God loves you and is going to help you achieve your best, and things will instantly be better. Business tapes are normally a great way to get a lot done while you are in the car, but when you have a problem that is all-consuming, it is difficult to stay on course. However, if the tape series covers solutions to the particular problem you are experiencing, then that would be the exception.

Exercise is always the best medicine. Sustained aerobic exercise will produce endorphins, which will automatically make us feel better. If you can add one hour of aerobic exercise every day, the size of your problem will decrease—guaranteed.

In any case, you need to proceed as quickly as possible in finding the solution to your problem. There may be a tendency to freeze; to not know what to do when a problem arises. You may feel sorry or hurt that the problem has occurred. It's so easy to drive ourselves crazy with the what-ifs and if-onlys, isn't it?

The sooner the better, we all need to snap out of it and start working directly on the problem. As soon as you determine a point of activity, start working on it immediately. As energy is put into the solution, more ideas and points of leverage will present themselves. This will give you further understanding of the solution. There may be the tendency to do everything yourself. Part of this is therapeutic, but eventually you just need to get work done to solve the problem. Get help for the things you can delegate, and focus on your strengths for your specific tasks. Every night before going to bed, write down a list of things that have to be accomplished during the next twenty-four hours. This will serve at least two purposes: first, you will be able to focus you energies directly on the problem the first thing in the morning; second, you will not wake yourself up in the night trying to remember everything you have to do tomorrow. It is also important to have a supply of paper and a pen close to you at night, for it is not unusual to wake up with a solution to part of the problem you are experiencing. You can then quickly write it down and get back to sleep. Otherwise, sleep may not come easily because you may worry if you will remember the solution in the morning.

You need to relax, to get away for awhile, when you are actively problem solving. Try to do something you are passionate about that will consume your mind completely. Go and get an extra-long massage. Have a steam bath, or get a facial. All of these things will give you a chance to relax and get away for a short time.

I have a little way of relaxing, which I learned when I was in college. I learned to do it after I read about self-hypnotism. I try to lie in a very comfortable place; it does not have to be in bed. I close my eyes and try to relax. Then I start at the tips of my toes and imagine that part of me is relaxing. When I feel it, I move on to my foot. I repeat this process for my entire body. When I am done, then I visualize a place where I was totally relaxed. For me, this is a place in Florida when I was a teenager. Actually, after several hurricanes, this exact beach and pass are not there anymore. It is now exists only in my mind. I think of the place. I see it. I feel the warmth of the sun, the smell of the surf. I see myself cast a fishing line with a bobber attached to it. I see the bobber float along the sandy beach and over an area where I know there is sea grass under the water and a sea trout may be lurking. I know it must be an outgoing tide because of the way the bobber is moving. I see the trees and hear the breeze moving through them. I dwell on this vision, relaxing myself more and more. Even if I do not sleep, I will tell myself that I am rested. Using this technique, whether I sleep or not, I will have renewed energy to tackle the next task in solving my difficult situation.

After working on the problem and finding that you have reached an impasse, it might be time to call in an expert, mentor, or coach. Most times, people who have been through a personal or financial problem themselves are more than happy to help you when asked. If you do ask for someone's help, you need to provide that individual with information about your previous efforts. You need to show the person what you have done and ask for advice on your next move. This can save both of you countless hours. Obviously, this person has already been through a similar difficult time, and he can show you what worked for him. He may also supply you with resources for additional help. Sometimes this visit will guide you in a way you may not have considered.

It is essential for us to get over the negative things that happen in our lives and to seek positive benefits. This is a key concept so that we can move forward always. Sometimes it is very difficult to find the positive, but it is a fundamental goal in recovering from the problem, moving on, and making things better.

I have to share with you that, as I was writing this book for the first time, I was very excited. I had a lot of energy, and ideas flowed, and the work went on very quickly. I was amazed at how I was getting this project done, and it looked like I would be finished with the initial draft within a week. Due to my excitement, I left the computer on, and I would sit down and work whenever I had a few spare minutes. Well, a problem occurred with the computer, and it shut down unexpectedly. Overwhelmed with excitement for this project, I had not saved the work! When the computer was restarted, the project was on auto-save on the word processing program. When I went to recover it, the file was no longer there. I took the computer to a software expert, and the files could not be recovered. What a setback! But I just went with the idea that many successful people use after they lose fortunes—they know they have the knowledge and ability to make another. With this project, I knew I still had the knowledge in my head, and I could just bring it back into written form. In my search for the meaning of this occurrence, I have come to accept that I am now rewriting this work to make it better and more useful for you. The time I am spending now will be paid back in benefits for someone else, and somehow this experience will reward me in some way.

Many times our world does not seem to make sense. After working on a problem, we cannot find a way out of the dilemma in which we find ourselves. It is time for prayer. Personally, I find that when I offer up a problem up to God I have worked on, and admit that I do not presently have the ability to solve it, the solution many times has found me. There is a great power in this quiet time. Prayer does not have to be made in church. Simply taking the time to pray and acknowledge that God is in charge, no matter what happens, is the best tool we have available to us. Releasing our fears and concerns to God with complete faith in him always feels so liberating, and he always provides us with guidance and assistance in some way.

We have to be expecting a new idea, hunch, or feeling so that it can properly enter our thoughts. The important thing is that when this inspiration comes to us, we must act on it immediately. It may be a direct solution to the problem. It is crucial for us to solve the problem right then. There can be no solution without this application of the idea. There may be someone with whom we must meet to explain the solution to us—seek that person out! The solution may be knowledge in the form of a book—read it! There is a story in the Bible about a man named Job. Job loses everything. His fortune, his land, and his family are all gone. He never gives up on God. In the end, because of his unwavering belief, he is rewarded with many multiples of everything that was lost.

A letter to Paul

"Effort only fully releases its reward after
a person refuses to quit!" Napoleon Hill

Dear Paul,

I have been asked to visit with you for a
short while about the power of perseverance.
Certainly you are aware of the dictionary
meaning of the word, but between us, it
means the ability to never give up. It is the
will to do or the will to be. When you know
that you want something, you will search and
search for ways to make it happen.
Sometimes it may appear that you have
reached a brick wall with no way around, but
your constant work will uncover new ways of
solving a problem.

When I was in college, I still
remember working through some very
difficult physics problems. The professor
would give us the problems, but he would
also give us the answers. All we had to do
was come up with the solution to the
problem that would give that one correct
answer. We would work and work and still

not arrive at a way to get to the answer. Many times I would just be staring at the paper with no clue of how to proceed. A possible path to solve the equation would come to me. I would work through it, and it would not yield the right answer. I would go back through it to make sure that I did not have an error in my math. No, that was not the way to do it! More thought and time would be expended. A new way would come to mind. But then when it was tested, the wrong answer would come out of the lines of mathematical language. Maybe it was time to give up?

At this point, it was time to consult with other people who were trying to solve the same problem. Their attempts were different! There were different insights and different ways of navigating through the problems. After we each had explained what we had attempted, new synthesized methods were developed. The path from the problem to the solution was elusive. Again, an apparent wall had been reached. Totally frustrated with the lack of results, we would set the problem aside. Then, either while working on something totally unrelated, or during a moment of relaxation, the solution would come to mind. Back to the piece of paper and, as if a miracle had occurred, all the needed pieces of information were there.

How could this be—that the answer would just appear? Some people would say that it was the subconscious mind working on the solution and then sending the information to the conscious mind. Others would say that our minds were tapping into an electrical energy that contains all the known information in the universe. This universal intelligence is apparently available to all of us, if we only seek quiet and expect it to help us. Universal intelligence is also used to attempt to explain why a once-unsolvable problem can be solved at several different places in the world within a day of each other. Between us, Paul, I know that it is God. In the secret, quiet areas of our lives, God can show us solutions to our most difficult problems. We cannot expect the answer to come without work. We have to try and try again to find the answer ourselves and then, when we are sure we have given every way a try, if we admit that this problem is beyond us, God will show us the new way. You have to expect the answer and to work immediately on it as soon as the hunch, idea, or feeling comes to you. This may be a direct answer to the problem. It may lead you to someone who can help you understand what you need to do—seek them out! It may lead you to a book—read it! Paul, I hope this monologue will be useful to you. I am always here for you if you need me in any way. I am now going to leave you with a story I wrote about myself that you may find entertaining and useful.

Wishing you only the best!

Dr. Len Anglis

The Phenomenon

Phenomenon is a movie starring John Travolta as a man stricken by a great light and driven to the ground. During the following weeks, he realizes he can do incredible things. He is able to read and comprehend books in minutes, learn languages in mere hours, perform kinesis, and solve the problems of the world. The people of his town view him as strange. Many think he has been given powers by an alien being. As the story progresses, though, he is diagnosed with a brain tumor that will soon kill him. The tumor places pressure on the brain in a way that stimulates it and allows the hero to do amazing things.

A neurosurgeon wants to perform surgery to investigate the tumor and its effect on the brain. The hero refuses to take the risk of surgery. He wants to stay alive as long as possible to demonstrate the full potential of the brain.

Think of it. We all know we utilize less than 20 percent of our brain's potential. What would things be like if we used 30 percent, 40 percent, or 100 percent? What could we accomplish? What is holding us back that we *can* control?

To unlock our potential, I think the first thing we should do is observe others. What are they accomplishing? Who has set records? Who is doing the most? Who is doing something best? If someone else is doing it, you can, too. Find out how they do it, and do what they do to accomplish the same result.

A five-year-old patient of mine was recently diagnosed with leukemia. We felt badly about this but didn't know what to do to help. The next week, a flyer came across my desk looking for runners to raise funds for the Leukemia Society. I didn't hesitate, but I was miserably out of shape and overweight. I thought I'd have to walk the course. At an initial meeting, someone said that if I could run a certain distance within two months, I could sign up for a four-month training program for the marathon. Knowing people with severe physical disabilities have completed marathons, I thought that I should be able to do so, too.

Now, I am asking you to think about where you can stretch your potential. Why not run a marathon? Why not double your income? Why not contribute an unusually large amount of money to an organization? Why not write a book or give a lecture? Why not become an expert on a topic? It is said that one hour of study a day will make you an expert in three to five years.

Writing down goals can help us reach our potential. Even when we are not actively working on a goal, our minds are seeking solutions to the problems that impede our progress. Our goals may be layered and attached to each other. If we have several goals that are related, working on one goal may advance another. In my case, the goals of raising money for a good cause, running a marathon, attaining good health, and losing weight were all related. When doing something good for someone else is a component of our goals, we are more motivated. Our goals are more significant, more meaningful, and because of this motivation, more possible.

Sometimes as we work to accomplish our goals, other aspects of our lives improve and secondary goals are met. For example, in my case, when I committed to the marathon, I had to spend a lot of time running. As I ran, my health and energy rose, enabling me to meet the demands of my office, which at the time were considerable. The amazing thing was that I found that I had new time for my family and other business ventures, plus my practice production totals rose to record levels. As the running continued, I found myself pursuing a well-balanced set of many goals and making quick progress on all of them.

I think goals should be big—even huge. By stretching to do something big, we use more of our potential. Additionally, small goals do not force us to plan, and it is easy to procrastinate. When a goal is large, we break down the work and tend to start immediately. In the case of a marathon, the running training takes months, and I had to start immediately in order to fulfill my commitment. I say shoot for the moon! Even if you fail, you'll be among the stars.

There are always exceptional people who finish way before others. And there are always people who drop out along the way. For example, during the marathon, some people who had problems that impeded their progress dropped out rather than clock a poor time.

Little worries interfere with our resolve in every endeavor. It's happened to all of us, but I think we must persevere. Life, like a marathon, is sometimes a struggle. We have to pace ourselves to get to the finish. Many of us would rather work our way through trying times than quit. It's not so much how fast we finish, but how we finish.

If we sprint in the beginning but are unable to finish, there is no success. I've observed that slow, steady progress, even with time out to handle adversity, will bring us to the desired finish line. I would like to think that the turtle would beat the hare every time.

As my friend Dean and I ran the race, people recognized our Team Leukemia shirts and cheered us on. There were crowds waiting for someone they knew in the race and to cheer for them. Since we had aligned ourselves with an organization for others in need, many people cheered for us and gave us motivation to pick up our heads and keep pushing. In every endeavor, there will be people cheering at the beginning.

After eighteen miles, just as the race was starting to get the best of us, there were no crowds. We felt very alone, and even the scenery was no longer pleasant. The surroundings and our outlook were bleak. Isn't almost every large endeavor like this? At some point, you are in it all by yourself. We had run a long way but still had a long way to go. If we stopped now, we couldn't pick up next week where we stopped. When the next opportunity came around, we'd be at the starting line—with knowledge gained from this experience to help with the pace, but still starting over.

As we came over the final hill, we could see the finish line, and my eyes filled with tears of joy. I had rehearsed this joy of the finish in my mind many times. I looked over at my friend. Now, his sense of accomplishment was as important to me as my own.

Even when you don't have a record time, everyone cheers. As in life, everyone who finishes receives a medal. Just as we were twenty yards from the finish line, we saw our families and received a personal cheer.

It's an interesting phenomenon that when someone accomplishes a big goal, others are inspired to follow with the same performance. Previously, the attainment of this goal may have been thought an impossible feat. A perfect example is Roger Bannister breaking the four-minute mile for the first time. The following year, several others did the same. Many people have told me that next year, they are going to join my team and finish their first marathon.

I believe we should try to break a four-minute mile or run a marathon in dentistry. Break through a barrier and show others what is possible. I stay in my small office in a small town to prove to myself and others that the style of dentistry taught at the Pankey Institute can be practiced anywhere. When other people see what I accomplish, they will know it is possible for them. We need to raise the bar or carve a new benchmark, and then share it with others.

I've learned that when you see others accomplishing your goal, you know it can be done. Your challenge is to find out what they did and do the same!

As he finishes his lectures, Dr. Harold Wirth looked upon the dentists in the room and said that he knew each represented a dental family of approximately two thousand people. If he could help each dentist in the room provide even a little bit better care for their patients, it would be extremely gratifying. What gratifies you? What challenges will you meet? What will you make possible that was once thought impossible? I hope you reach your potential and become the next phenomenon.

The Bad and the Ugly

Are we really and truly interested in other people's problems? Most times people who talk about their problems are just venting. I have found that many people do not even listen to the advice given regarding their problems. In this instance, I am going to talk about a few of the things that have happened to me, to first share how I worked through them, but also so that I might have some credibility in what I tell you later. One of the first things that happened to me early in my career was that I purchased my dad's dental practice in January of 1983. As I made the transition into ownership, I took my insurance policies to my local agent to examine them. Unfortunately, all the insurance agent was interested in selling me was a life insurance policy. One month later, a fire broke out in my newly purchased office. What a mess! Most of the contents were destroyed, and what was left had been damaged from the smoke and heat. Then I learned that the insurance covered only the building, and very little was paid for the contents. I had some very expensive pieces of equipment that needed to be replaced, and there was no insurance to help.

I think I lost over twelve pounds the first couple days. There were so many things to consider. Should I move the office and start over in a different location? What was I going to do with all the damaged equipment? How was I going to get the office building back in a usable condition? What was I going to do for the people who worked for me? What were they going to do? Would I have work for them to do? Would I have to lay them off? The list of questions seemed to be endless, and my list of answers was initially empty. To say the least, I was very confused. As I have alluded to earlier in this text, my mind was spinning out of control. Somehow I had to find a place to start and get a plan to complete this project.

The initial long-range goal was to get the office back together and working as soon as possible. Trying to limit a decrease in income during that time was my primary intention. The first projects involved closing up the structure. Then, finding what was still acceptable for use as far as equipment and building materials, and getting rid of what could not be salvaged. This plan involved totally rebuilding the interior and also performing any needed repairs on the outside while the building was unoccupied. I repaired the equipment that hadn't been damaged too badly and replaced everything else. I rented space across the street and rented equipment to allow me to see patients on a limited basis while also overseeing the construction process. The end result was that my office was back in business in less than three months. I believe that I was able to get through this time because I always focused on what the end result was going to be. It was very important at that time to have goals for each day. By outlining every step, I was able to be very efficient with time. I also had support from my family and friends.

The financial issue also seemed to resolve itself. I got an unexpected refund from the government. I got more insurance payments than I thought possible. My house, which had been for sale for several months without an offer, sold for full price and brought me a needed profit. Additionally, I was able to sell a sports car I had to help raise funds to pay off the project. Finally, since I was able to continue to work from the temporary office that I set up, I had a limited income from that source. The office ended up being designed properly and has served me well for the past thirty years!

Don't Tread on Me

We all know and cherish the thought that we live in a free country. Somehow when you get a letter from the Internal Revenue Service, this thought seems to evaporate relatively quickly. The problem was compounded when the accountant who had been taking care of the books was away on vacation. I looked at the letter, and it was a daunting letter indeed. The letter outlined that they were going to essentially go through all of my records for one year with the threat that they may need to investigate further in the past. My philosophy in business has always been not to cheat anyone, particularly the government and its taxation process. This cheating would create problems that could not be fixed. I tried to look for justification for deductions for my business. Some might call this an aggressive form of tax planning. On top of that, I had been extremely busy and wasn't taking care of my record keeping as was directed. I would have a receipt that I knew I should hang on to, but since so many years had elapsed, and no one had asked for them, many receipts just got filed in the garbage. So when I got the letter, I was instantly terrified. Since my tax professional was out of touch, I did not have anyone to consult with regarding my situation. In a fervent attempt to do something, I took home the records, which were not organized, and this did not help my mental state at all!

When I finally got to talk to my accountant, he was able to outline a strategy for the initial meeting. The first idea was to try to relocate the audit to the city where my accountant's office was located. But there was absolutely no give in the investigator on anything. Since it was nearly impossible to provide all the documentation the letter requested, the accountant's plan was to come to the first meeting with some working papers and the entire checkbook registry. The agent examined the books during the morning and then outlined the areas that needed further documentation. The documentation required was substantial, but it was nowhere near as much as the initial letter outlined. Fortunately, we live in the computer age, and almost all the invoices and statements that were necessary were reproducible. Quickly, I found that it was a sort of game to try and please the agent. Where the deductions were not clear, we wrote narratives to explain the reason why we were deducting a certain expense. When we found mistakes, we were very clear to point them out, and explain how they would be corrected in the future.

Did I worry about the outcome? Of course I did! Then I started to do worst-case scenario. Would I go to jail for anything that I reported on my income tax form? No! Not even close. Would I have to pay more tax? Maybe. Would there be interest and maybe a penalty? Probably. I came up with a number that I thought it might be and developed a potential plan for taking care of the extra tax. This mental plan had a little kink in it when I got a letter from the IRS stating that they were disallowing my deductions and that over $300,000 was due in back taxes for that year. The initial reading of this letter took the blood right out of my face! After looking at it closer, I realized that this was their way to get the necessary documentation in by a certain day. Part of their sick game. There were many sleepless nights, but I kept reminding myself of the worst-case scenario. If I hadn't comforted myself with the truth, my mind would have traveled to places where everything would have gotten amplified. After about four months of worry about what was going to happen because of this audit, I found out that I did not owe any extra taxes at all. Of course, I had a big bill from the people who represented me in this issue.

Judas, DDS

Nearly everyone has lost a friend or a loved one. This doesn't have to be a clinical death, since a loss due to a misunderstanding or a lack of truthfulness can be just as devastating. I had a friend who I worked with on many projects. I always considered him to be one of my best friends. We joined forces to get trained together to do certain procedures in our offices. During that training process, I helped him find suitable patients and also provided some of the treatment for those patients at no charge so that he could have the best training. I lent him equipment, helped train his staff, and even explained upcoming treatment to his patients. There were plans for us to go into business together to provide a very innovative and sophisticated form of treatment.

Everything was going great with the formation of our partnership. And then, all of a sudden, the whole thing fell apart, and initially, I was shocked. I had always wondered why my friend spent time with a couple other doctors who had questionable motives, but I overlooked it as a quirk. It is my belief that it was the jealously of either one or both of these other professionals which undermined my business and personal relationship with my friend. Over a couple years time a relationship which I thought to be closer to me than a brother had disintegrated into something which resembled an opponent in a gladiator event. Finally I was informed by certified mail that I could no longer be part of his educational opportunities at his office. This was especially disturbing to me because he had always been included in the same opportunies sponsored by my office. I really could not believe that this had happened. It was as if the person I considered to be like a brother had been replaced by an evil twin. How had I been tricked? Certainly I had to find something positive in this situation. I had the solace that God had put this challenge in front of me to prepare me for something very special.

I know now that I have to always be aware to spot new opportunities that come my way. The lesson that I immediately learned was that I was not tricked. This person had shown who he was by his relationships with other people and by how he treated other professionals. I had plenty of signs to show me who I was really with, but I chose to look away from these. In the future, I need to trust my intuition since it will never mislead me.

My wife asked me why that traitor lied to us. I think the late motivational speaker Jim Rohn had it right: The person had no choice in the matter, for he is a liar. What would you expect a liar to do? Liars lie. You can't expect a cheater to do anything but cheat. Robbers rob; whiners whine. Growing up I had heard the story of the scorpion and the frog many times. It was not until this turn of events that I fully understood its full meaning.

The Story of the Scorpion and the Frog

One day, a scorpion looked around at the mountain where he lived and decided that he wanted a change. So he set out on a journey through the forests and hills. He climbed over rocks and under vines and kept going until he reached a river.

The river was wide and swift, and the scorpion stopped to reconsider the situation. He couldn't see any way across. So he ran upriver and then checked downriver, all the while thinking that he might have to turn back.

Suddenly, he saw a frog sitting in the rushes by the bank of the stream on the other side of the river. He decided to ask the frog for help getting across the stream.

"Hello, Mr. Frog!" called the scorpion across the water. "Would you be so kind as to give me a ride on your back across the river?"

"Well now, Mr. Scorpion! How do I know that if I try to help you, you won't try to kill me?" asked the frog hesitantly.

"Because," the scorpion replied, "if I try to kill you, then I would die too, for you see, I cannot swim!"

Now this seemed to make sense to the frog. But he asked, "What about when I get closer to the bank? You could still try to kill me and get back to the shore!"

"This is true," agreed the scorpion. "But then I wouldn't be able to get to the other side of the river!"

"Alright, then … but how do I know you won't just wait till we get to the other side and *then* kill me?" said the frog.

"Ah," crooned the scorpion. "Because you see, once you've taken me to the other side of this river, I will be so grateful for your help that it would hardly be fair to reward you with death, now would it?"

So the frog agreed to take the scorpion across the river. He swam over to the bank and settled himself near the mud to pick up his passenger. The scorpion crawled onto the frog's back, his sharp claws prickling into the frog's soft hide, and the frog slid into the river. The muddy water swirled around them, but the frog stayed near the surface so the scorpion would not drown. He kicked strongly through the first half of the stream, his flippers paddling wildly against the current.

Halfway across the river, the frog suddenly felt a sharp sting in his back and, out of the corner of his eye, saw the scorpion remove his stinger from the frog's back. A deadening numbness began to creep into his limbs.

"You fool!" croaked the frog. "Now we shall both die! Why on earth did you do that?"

The scorpion shrugged, and did a little jig on the drowning frog's back.

"I could not help myself. It is my nature."

Then they both sank into the muddy waters of the swiftly flowing river.

Procrastination: The Big Thief

Procrastination is one of the major evils in our lives that will slow us down and prevent us from accomplishing our goals. People who look at all the things that I have in the works have said that they cannot believe that I would be worried about such a thing. It seems that I have become so good at procrastination that you can look at me and not even know that I am doing it.

There are constantly projects that need to be started and accomplished. We need techniques to make sure we stay on course with what we intend to do. It is a well-known fact that at least 80 percent of our effort goes into creating only 20 percent of our results. We may actually be less productive than this ratio suggests, because today a great amount of time is spent procrastinating by technological means. I know it is hard to resist looking at e-mails, seeing how many people are on Twitter or Facebook, or spending other nonproductive time on the computer. What we need to do is to identify the 20 percent that gets us our results and starting spending a majority of our time on those practices. It is important to identify the most significant task that has the potential to get us a big result and to work on it first. It may be the research that we have to do or the difficult phone call that we dread making. This should be the very first thing that we do. After it is done, our minds will be released from the mental bondage that the procrastination has inflicted upon us. We will be far more effective during the day.

The very successful people that I know use different tricks or games to motivate themselves. Dan Kennedy, a very successful entrepreneur and copywriter, will place a check that a client has paid him for his expertise on the pile of work that has to be completed to earn that check. He does not cash the check until the work in the pile is finished. Seeing the money sitting there waiting for him gives him the motivation to keep on the project until it is finished. Personally, I get more work done if I think of every week as a week right before I leave on vacation.

I'm Going on Vacation

I have often noticed that the week before I go away, my outlook, perspective, and energy levels change. The start of this transformation begins after I have defined and written down a list of all the things that must be accomplished before I go. As each task is accomplished, it is systematically checked off of the list. I will dictate all correspondences and complete all lab work, and the cases that must go out are boxed and sent away. Patients who are in the midst of treatment are called to make sure they are feeling comfortable. All business phone calls are made, all bills are paid, and the information that needs to be sent to the accountant is put in the mail. This ritual is so well known at my office that even the week before, my staff prepares to get set for all the extra things that will be delegated or assigned during this time. Patient treatment goes extremely well, and consultations that are presented during this week are accepted. The energy is so concentrated that we are able to complete an incredible amount of work. By the end of the week, both my desk and lab bench are completely cleared.

Simultaneously, all preparations at home are made, including all of the shopping for the trip. Then the packing starts. My wife starts laughing as soon as she thinks about me doing this, because I literally take everything out of the closet and the dressers and try it on. I will then make a decision as to whether I am going to keep the item or not. If not, they are put into the bag for charity. So, in essence, my closets and drawers are reorganized every time I leave. We do not leave until the house is completely clean, so that when we come home we only have laundry to face.

In this short time before a trip, we accomplish things that have we've delayed doing for months or possibly even since the last trip. At the office and at home, everything is accomplished and completed. When I look at my productivity and receivables at the office, these numbers are not affected by my leaving. If anything, they may have increased. Just wait a minute! I work 25 percent less, and I produce the same. Usually I spend a couple days wondering how much I could accomplish if I could keep up this initiative and concentration throughout the year. But when I return home, it is back to my normal routine again.

But seriously, what if we considered each week as if it were the week before a vacation? Instead of going to the airport at the end of the week, we go home. I started thinking about my week just like that. When you really reflect on the reasons why the week preceding vacation is so successful, it can be attributed to preparation, even before the week begins. I know exactly what I have to complete. Yes, I *do* have goals prepared before *every* week starts. Ideally, this should be the last task completed before leaving for the weekend. This would then afford the subconscious mind the entire weekend to design the best way to achieve everything.

To accomplish treatment more efficiently, I spend additional time in the morning planning out the day and mentally treating every patient. Before the start of the day, I set up the lab with all the materials needed throughout the day in sequential order. This is a tremendous time-saver and adds to the quality of my care..

Keeping up with my reading has always been a problem. I try to stay on top of this by tearing out articles from journals that I specifically want to read and throwing the rest of the journal away. I carry these articles with me so I can read them when I have some extra time. Evelyn Wood's Reading Dynamics course says that in a one-day course they can triple your reading speed and increase your retention dramatically. What if reading speed was only doubled?

Letter writing has always been a problem, so instead of physically sitting down and writing by hand or using a word processor, I now dictate all my letters. This saves a tremendous amount of time for me and for my business manager—she doesn't have to come to me trying to figure out what I have written down. Finally, I take the phone with me during the drive home. Instead of just listening to music, I can make the follow-up calls to patients. I also have my tapes available so I can listen to lectures I was unable to attend, or motivational tapes to maintain my attitude. You know these ideas are not new. You have heard them a thousand times. It is just a matter of implementing them.

For me, the thought that the end of the week is actually the beginning of a vacation puts a closure on the week. It puts limits on the goals I have set for this segment of time. Every week when I leave with work having been cleared from my desk and lab, I have a real sense of satisfaction. Instead of carrying this work home with me to work on, as I did before, I can be more effective with my family on the weekend. I have been adhering to this technique for the last several months, and the results have been fantastic. I am planning for an incredible increase in my practice this year, and I have also decided to accomplish a lot of writing and reading, as well as participating more fully in organized dentistry. Along with this, I am planning more free time with my family this year. It *will* be a more common sight to see the limo pulling up to my drive and me with a big smile on my face, thinking, "I'm going on vacation!"

Vapors of Time

From time to time, someone will ask me how many hours I have in a day. This is usually accompanied by disbelief that I am taking on another project or finishing another paper. Personally, I feel like I could be doing a lot more. It seems that for the most part, I am coasting. If I had to, I could really step on the gas and get somewhere! I prove this to myself every time I impose a time limitation on the completion of a goal or project. Invariably, everything gets done. Why? Because I have established a set of goals, and when I finish one, I work on finishing the next.

We have tasks that must be done throughout the day, but there is always a spare moment. When I reach one of these times, I find it very effective to have in front of me written notes about a project or task on which to focus my energy.

We need to creatively look for time throughout the day to achieve our goals. Because I remain a Chicago Bulls fan who is still in denial about what happened to what was once a championship team, I continuously reminisce about the Michael

Jordan days. One of his talents as a basketball player was his ability to approach the opposing team's defense and see things happening in a way that would allow him to successfully predict how things would play out in the next few seconds. When he made his move, there seemed to be a superhighway opening up in the lane where, in a split-second more, there would be only defenders. I'm sure this happened in slow motion to Michael, but it was a blur to everyone else. We need to be like him in order to see open moments of time and act on them.

Time is like gasoline that is dropped on the pavement. If left undisturbed, it will vaporize and the pavement will quickly dry, leaving no trace of gasoline behind. But before it vaporizes, if we put a spark to it, the gasoline will ignite. There will be an explosion and a fire. Writing down a goal with a specific completion date can be the spark that ignites openings in time before they evaporate.

Written goals are as simple as a list of things to do. They can be educational, monetary, spiritual, relational, recreational, and so on. Once we have goals on our list, we should prioritize them. What is most important? What is least important? These simple steps will almost always ensure some success. To create a surefire plan, we should then take each of the goals and work through all of the steps necessary to accomplish them. A schedule should be applied to the steps.

I find it is best to read my schedule of milestones twice a day. I read mine on rising each morning, to fix in my mind my objectives for the day. I read them again before retiring at night, to allow my subconscious, during sleep, to work on problems associated with the attainment of my goals. Many times I wake up suddenly during the night with the answer to a problem.

We cannot expect to accomplish great things in each short snippet of time, but the cumulative effect of these, day after day, will multiply our results. Just converting fifteen minutes per day into productive time will equate to an additional ninety-one hours per year to allow us to accomplish our goals. A half hour of study a day for three to five years will make you an expert on any subject. This small change in how we look at time will increase our accomplishments to the extent that people will wonder if we sleep at all.

As we perfect our visualization of time, we will see more that we can use. People around us will be looking frayed, and our previous efforts will pay off like a pump that has been primed—with little effort at the handle, water flows and flows. Our days will seem to slow up and provide endless opportunities.

At this time, I would like you to remember the words of Dr. Harold Wirth: "Life is like an hourglass. We cannot be sure of how much sand is in the top of our hourglass, but as sure as we are sitting here, these grains of sand are continually moving from the top to the bottom, never to be reclaimed again. Of all the moments of recorded history, there is only one today with opportunities that will never be presented again. As we grow older and more of the grains of sand have passed through the hourglass, they become more valuable to us. Please do not waste your precious grains of sand!"

Lifestyle

Whenever lifestyle is mentioned, we tend to think of the show, *Lifestyles of the Rich and Famous*, don't we? Many times, shows such as this one aren't so much about the lifestyle of a celebrity as they are a chronicle of all the stuff he or she owns. This in no way constitutes a lifestyle. Lifestyle is more about using what you have to craft a great life for yourself and your family. What kind of lifestyle would it be for you to be able to purchase a large, luxurious home for your family, but because you are so busy with your business, you are never home to enjoy it? Or you are under great stress to produce an income to afford those large payments? Crafting a lifestyle is like creating an experience for everyone around you.

A very successful executive from New York City was on vacation in a small Mexican village. He was present as a fisherman docked his small boat, filled with three exceptional tuna he had caught. The executive was amazed by the catch, and asked the fisherman how long it took him to catch the fish. The fisherman responded that it did not take him very long. A conversation ensued.

"Why didn't you stay and catch more fish?"

"This is all the fish that my family can use."

"What are you going to do with the rest of the day?"

"I have a very busy day. I am going to get something to eat, play with my kids, and then take a nap. When I wake, I will go to the village and drink some wine, play the guitar, and sing and visit with my friends."

The executive said the fisherman should stay out longer, catch more fish, and sell them in the marketplace. With the proceeds, he could buy a bigger boat to catch more fish.

"Then what?" asked the fisherman.

"Then you can buy a more boats until you have a fleet of boats, with many people working for you."

"Then what?" asked the fisherman.

"Then you will first have to move to Mexico City, then LA, and then finally to New York, to run your giant international fishing operation."

"Then what?" asked the fisherman.

"You then will be able to make a public offering of your company on the New York Stock Exchange, and then you will make millions."

"Millions? What will I do then?"

"You will retire to a small Mexican village, where you can sleep in late, fish when you want, play with your kids, drink wine, and play your guitar."

You Must Choose,
but Choose Wisely!

Lifestyle involves some choices. I love to spend time on vacation with my entire family. My kids always go with us. We have traveled to some exclusive locations, and I am so happy that everyone is with me to experience those places, but more important, we are all together. We have some our best memories as a family from our trips together. When we travel, I let the kids experience the best in entertainment. I remember taking my kids to see the Three Tenors (Pavarotti, Domingo, and Carreras). People around could not believe that we paid full price for small children to see the performance. Although they do not remember the whole performance, it may serve as an association for appreciation in the future. It was very important for me to have them there to witness the performance. It was also important to me to express to others that my children were so important that they should be there for that performance. This is an important part of my lifestyle.

I differ from a lot of my acquaintances, who would never take their children with them on an important vacation or to an expensive performance. I will invest in this experience, but a trade-off is that I have not purchased a factory-new car in over twenty years. I let someone else use the car for the first year to allow me to buy it for half the price of a new car. Many times warranties are available for used cars that are far superior to those available for new cars. So I choose one thing over another. I know that for some people, the new car is the important thing, but I must caution you not to spend on something that will be gone in five years when you can invest in memories with your family that will last a lifetime. Trips might involve plane tickets that are upgraded with saved miles. Hotel stays have been complimentary through points accumulated on credit card accounts. The end result is still something special. Time invested with my family which will pay dividends for years.

The Cat's in the Cradle

Lifestyle might also include working hard at work to complete all the tasks for the day so that when you get home, you are all at home and not half at work. I know many people who bring projects from work home with them and end up ignoring their spouses and families. Try to work at work, and be at home or on vacation when appropriate. The father continues to come home every night with a big pile of work from the office. Day after day the little boy wants to play catch with his father. Every day the reply is the same: son, I have to get my work done from the office. One day, in frustration, the little boy goes to his mother and wonders if dad is always going to bring home work from the office. The mom sighs and says that for dad to keep up, he has to bring home the work. The little boy responds by saying that, at his school, if you cannot keep up, they put you in a slower group.

We need to put ourselves in with a slower group if we cannot keep up with our obligations at home. Certainly we have times that we need to put in extra time on a project, but it has to be something very important that will reap us great returns. In these cases, we need to have a meeting with the family so that they understand what we are up against, and that when it has been completed, there will be payback time. Time repaid with compound interest. If you do this too often, you will get yourself behind with your family, and there may not be enough time to catch up. Allow yourself to stay current with your family.

Endorphins, Anyone?

Another essential ingredient that must be incorporated into a healthy lifestyle is the time to enjoy physical activity. Personally, I find it very difficult to go to the gym and work out on machines there. Now, a wild game of tennis or an invigorating bicycle ride, and you are speaking my language! A hike up a trail or cross-country skiing, and I am right there alongside you! For the busy person, one hour a day for five days is integral to keeping up your good health. The benefits of regular exercise abound, including improvement of cardiovascular health, disease prevention, better overall mood due to increased endorphin activity— the list goes on and on. Like spending time with your family, you can get caught up in placing your exercise needs on a low priority rung. If you let too much time go by, it gets harder and harder to get caught up. It is easy to do these things, but it is equally easy not to do them. Jim Rohn would say that you have to make a choice between the two easies. One of the easies yields the rewards of a life well lived. The other easy leads to a place of regret for not having achieved your potential.

Gratitude for Gratuity

Living a life well lived may take on other nuances that are not that big on the surface, yet yield an amazing return. There is an immediate feeling of happiness, but there is also a lingering feeling that encourages you to create more, be more, and to have more. What about purchasing a small gift for someone? Why not buy lunch for the people who are working around your house? Why not buy a small token for the teacher, the caretaker, the person of service to you who may be forgotten day in and day out? What an easy way to make someone's day—or week, or month.

The term *TIP* is an abbreviation of the words *to insure promptness*. Give some money to the person who goes to get your car. Instead of waiting for the end of the meal, why not give the server some money at the start of the meal and explain to him that you want his full attention to make it a night of nights? Why not give a little extra to men who work as valets at the hotel where you are staying for a week, and see how quickly they will run up to get the claim ticket to go get your car? If you are in a situation where two figures come to your head as an amount for a tip, always give the bigger tip. Of course the person will be appreciative of the money, but you will feel like a king in giving this amount. Certainly you do not want to take a chance on dwelling about how cheap you were in giving the smaller tip.

The other night, my wife, Nancy, and I were at a small tapas restaurant. Right next to us, a fellow was entertaining us on a classical guitar. He was quite good, and his performance was thoroughly entertaining. Nancy asked me if I was going to leave a tip for this fellow. The tip jar on the stage was begging to be fed, for the only occupants were a couple bent-up dollar bills. What kind of tip would a dollar be? I would say not much, not much at all. What would that say to performer? Certainly this was not a street performer. I told Nancy I was going to put in twenty dollars. That is a big tip, isn't it? Well, not for an hour-and-a-half performance for the two of us. Where could we get into a concert for ten dollars each? Dropping the bill in the jar, we saw the performer acknowledge the gesture. He knew that he had reached me on some level, and I was expressing appreciation for his skills. Just as important was the way the owner of the restaurant looked at the bill in the jar. I could see him thinking, "Maybe this guy should perform more often. I thought he was good, but now I know someone else does." I could feel that this would make a difference for a least a couple of people. I felt good in releasing that money that night. I felt good the next day in church when I prayed a prayer of thanks for the life and lifestyle that I was given. I do not think that if I had bought myself a new gold watch, I would have got the feeling that I got from that small gesture. What a value that was! All for just twenty dollars, certainly a small amount to invest. Do you think that I would have a better chance of being successful at whatever I do the next couple days because of the relatively small gesture I made?

Maestro, Raise Your Baton!

In the summer of 1999, we had the extreme good fortune to see, as a family, the Three Tenors (Pavarotti, Carreras, and Domingo) perform live at Tiger Stadium in Detroit. The afternoon had been rainy, and in our hotel room we watched the weather channel radar track an extremely large thunderstorm headed directly for the historic stadium. I changed from my dress shoes to my running shoes in preparation for the soaking we were about to receive. We arrived early and stood in line for this once-in-a-lifetime performance. When we were inside the stadium, we found that my Internet ticket-finding ability had been effective—we were on the field, close to the stage.

I kept looking skyward to check on the darkness and swirling winds. Just as the announcer finished telling us that all three performers were present and ready to perform, the sky began to clear, and the stars became visible, one by one. Then, each of the tenors came on stage, one after the other, and performed. The music filled the stadium and seemed to pick us up off our chairs. Even my five-year-old son was temporarily mesmerized by what was happening. Each of the tenors seemed to try to outdo the others.

Tension grew with each succeeding performance. Then, Luciano Pavarotti performed the piece "Nessun Dorma." The beauty of the piece and his interpretation brought everyone I could see to tears. They continued as a trio to perform several songs until the end of the program. At the conclusion, they were greeted by a continuous standing ovation through four encore pieces.

The music that night was technically perfect as far as I could assess, even though critics have said the three voices have had better days. But their technical perfection is not what brought everyone to their feet. It was their interpretation and emotion. It seemed evident to me that without the art of performance added to the science of music, these fabulous operas would be no more interesting than elevator music.

If we quickly change our thoughts to dentistry, we can view it also as an art just as much as a science. What if we were to emphasize the science over the art? Would the dentistry be lifeless? Of course it would.

Just as Pavarotti takes a lifeless piece of music—a scientific, mathematical equation—and creates a living emotional statement, shouldn't our dentistry reflect emotion?

The Emotional Side

I think our overemphasis on the technical aspect of dentistry, almost to the point of ignoring the emotional side of our work, leaves out the part that could add to the appreciation of our craft. I have heard patients calling offices for an initial exam, and the person in charge almost reads a script of what the doctor is going to accomplish at the first visit. This is followed by the fee that is due at the first appointment.

In my office, I have taken the person in charge of the front desk aside and asked a series of questions. You have been in several dental offices over your life, correct? What is different about the experience here that makes it special? Why was it important to have that first exam? Why should the patient look forward to it? How can you help someone remember the benefit received so they can explain it to someone else with enthusiasm? How can you help the patient realize this is what he or she really wants, so the patient looks forward to the experience?

When the patient arrives at the office, he or she should feel as though in a spa. The patient should be pampered and made to feel very special and important. There should be a healing atmosphere to the décor. Refreshments should be available for visitors. Everyone should be prepared as if company is coming for a special dinner in our home.

Using the methods developed at the Pankey Institute, we automatically give our attention to the patient during the initial interview. We have to educate, but more important, we must listen to the needs and expectations of the patient.

A patient stopped by our office to look around and requested some information on dental implants. The next day, the patient called and asked to have time to speak to me. During the ensuing appointment, the patient revealed her most intimate fears and the various reasons she had been avoiding dental treatment. She was concerned that the dentist and staff would look down upon her or criticize her for her oral condition. Her initial visit to the office to get information was her way of scouting to make sure no one who knew her worked here. After our visit, she knew we cared and were empathetic, and we knew to schedule her for her appointments on non-busy days and with always the same assistant.

The consultation appointment is one of the most important times to incorporate art and emotion. In making a large purchase, people will evaluate it on both an emotional and logical basis. The emotional content of the presentation sells the person, and it is the logical portion that the person typically uses to justify the purchase. Many times in a presentation, the dentist will emphasize the technical aspects of the treatment. Somehow, emotion has to be incorporated into this process. Whether it is excitement or emphasis on the benefits, it is this aspect that allows a patient to say yes. Yes! *Yes!*

When we give information to a patient, it is like the small pins found in shirts to hold them together in the package. If I throw the pins at you and they hit you on the hand or cheek, you will feel them. But if I take one of those pins and attach it to an iron bar, I can drive it through your heart. The pins are the logical information, and the bar is the emotion.

Throughout our careers, we will continuously study how to measure and use the emotional content effectively. Without the emotional mode, patients will not be able to feel the benefits of the treatment. When showing one patient an esthetic wax-up of her front teeth, I told her an artist took wax and fashioned her teeth in a way that would change her smile. Normally very reserved and professional, the lady broke into tears, saying that she had put up with her appearance her entire life and never felt she could smile. Now, she knew it would be possible. She wanted to start immediately. She had not yet received information about what was involved and what it would cost. With a precise idea of how we will feel or how we will look, we can justify the time, money, and discomfort to get there.

The Artistry

During treatment, we need to emphasize the artistic things we do. Once, a patient was referred by another to our office. She was told I was an "artistic" dentist. What had I done to give my patient the feeling that I was artistic? What could I do in the future to make sure more patients thought of me in that way? In my mind, artistry is one of the most important things we can accomplish to ensure patient satisfaction. Truthfully, though, I don't know the answer to these questions.

I have some notion of what can lead the patient to the assumption I am artistic. Use of our study models and the time we invest in making them is a start. We are sculptors when we fashion a lifelike replica out of acrylic. In theory, how much different can our instruments be than the tools used by Michelangelo to carve the statue of David? The porcelain artist uses various layers of color to fashion a replica of our provisional, and also uses the color to develop a lifelike, three-dimensional appearance. This can be compared to the fresco painter who rapidly places multiple layers of color before the plaster dries. We have to believe in our artistic talents and techniques. When we do, we can convey the sense that we are artistic to our patients.

During the post-case interview, we have our final chance to emphasize the emotion and the artistic content of our work. Usually, this is not necessary because the patient is already benefiting from the time and effort of our work. I recall one case where, after we finished taking the post-case pictures for a complete restoration, tears welled up into the eyes of the patient. She began to relate that she was sure when she started treatment that she would lose her remaining teeth. She was impressed by the time we spent educating her and then creating the result necessary to satisfy her concerns.

The Applause

What is the appropriate response to a compliment? Certainly, we need to acknowledge the compliment in some fashion. I have seen people in this situation say something like, "It was nothing." What a travesty—especially with something as complex as reconstructive treatment! I have never seen a performer not acknowledge the applause and appreciation. This applause is like the carbohydrates an endurance runner takes in after a long effort. Taking it all in is necessary for refueling and growing stronger for the next time.

Our work is something significant. It is something very special. We do it with genuine care and caring. It is our responsibility to charge the patient with becoming a missionary for this kind of treatment. The patient who has experienced the benefits and has the words to express the emotional benefits firsthand is a powerful promoter of dentistry. In a few words, a patient can motivate others to seek this type of care. The patient does not encourage others out of economic gain, but out of true gratitude. Encourage your satisfied patients to motivate others.

You are the conductor of the symphony of your practice and your life. Dental performances should be our emphasis in the treatment of our patients. We must tune in to our artistic side, because this is the side that contains the emotion.

When a patient started to cry at a post-case interview, she stated that she would love us forever because of the way her treatment had changed her life. This happened almost ten years ago, but I can still feel the emotion and appreciation given to me at that moment. Dr. Pankey would say the appreciation given for a case well done was far more important than the fee the patient paid. How true this is!

It is the appreciation that will drive us to the next level on our ladder of development. By making our treatment into a performance, our patients will travel great distances to experience our care. It is with this attitude I am sure you will hear applause and see tears of appreciation for your art. So it is with much pleasure and anticipation I command you, "Maestro, raise your baton!"

Goals

A goal is a personal discussion we have with ourselves to decide where we want to go. Together, they create our target. Today, things are moving so quickly that we can be carried along by chance. We could have the appearance of moving, but where are we going? In five or ten years, we arrive somewhere. Without a goal, we have no choice in where we end up. In five or ten years, we arrive somewhere. We may not like it there. Wouldn't it be better to choose our own destination?

It is important to follow your master plan in its appropriate order. If your goal was to see the Statue of Liberty and Ellis Island in New York, that would be a great start. You would be really motivated and tell everyone about it. Maybe someone has even promised you that you could write an article for their magazine and be compensated financially. You are excited as you get off the plane and into your rental car. Your map, though, is not labeled, and is actually a map of Los Angeles. No matter that you are motivated to reach your goal—

you do not have a good and accurate plan or map, and you will not get there! If you do get there, it will only be because of chance. So the next phase is to plan out every step of the way to your goal. What you need to do first, second, and third. If something unexpected happens during this progression, what will your alternative plan be? After some progress is made, the plan has to be reassessed to see if you are still heading in the right direction. On a trip to the moon, there are many mid-flight corrections to make up for unforeseen circumstances.

Motivation is the gasoline for success. Once you know where you are going and how you are going, motivation will take you there. We all have a certain amount of self-motivation. Some have more than others. Sometimes reading a book or going to a lecture will reenergize our spirits and refill our motivation tanks. Motivation comes to us from different sources. We need to identify our richest vein and tap into it on a regular basis to get to our destination as soon as possible.

Henry Ford was absolutely right in saying, "Whether you think you can or can't, you are right." It is up to us to create our own customized plan for success and to motivate ourselves towards its completion. Trust me on this one: there is nothing more exhilarating than being in complete charge of your destiny!

Hit the Bull's-Eye

As the New Year arrives, it is the perfect opportunity to ponder what has happened during the past year. Am I closer to or further away from my intended goals? What actions have created these consequences? Certainly, a person who learns from his or her failures is a success. More important, we should take all of this learning and reinvest it in the next year's opportunities.

One thing I want to do during this time of introspection is to challenge my beliefs about myself and what I am doing. Could I be more, do better, produce more? Has someone said something about me or dentistry that has changed my perspective? Has this changed perspective limited my potential?

When I finished my oral surgery rotation in my general practice residency, the head of the department wrote that I got along well with everyone and would do well in practice, but oral surgery would never be a big part of my practice! For some time I questioned this critique. This was only his opinion, so I just put it out of my mind. Yet in my early years in practice, I allowed this opinion to become my own. Whenever an oral surgery appointment was on the schedule, I started to think about it early in the day. Would I be able to get the tooth numbed enough? Would the tooth fracture? I remember often using a lot of extra time and effort in these procedures, totally messing up my schedule for the day. When I got busy with my restorative practice, Dr. Pankey hardly had to mention eliminating from your practice the things you don't like or can't do as well as you want.

Les Brown, a powerful motivational speaker, reminds us that "someone's opinion of you does not have to become your reality." If there is something that you want to do, but are not doing for whatever reason, look to those who *are* doing it; find out where and how they have learned to do so, and get that specific information. You can learn to do anything if you have the right mentor and you are willing to pay the price.

After I had been doing restorative treatment in my practice for awhile, I wanted to integrate implant treatment into my treatment plans. During my learning process, I had trouble communicating what I needed to the surgeon, and I ended up with implants in not exactly the right places. When the opportunity came to take a one-year surgical and prosthetic course in implant dentistry, I jumped at it. I had no intention of doing the surgery portion in my practice, but I wanted to do several surgeries to understand why I was not getting my desired results. During the course, I had a wonderful experience and found I could design and execute implant surgery and prosthetics quite well. Because of my success, many restorative dentists in the area have asked me to do the implant surgery for their patients.

Recently, I was completing a surgery at my friend's office. It involved removing a broken-down molar, removing an impacted canine, sinus elevation, and grafting of the extraction sites. These procedures were completed in less than an hour, without rushing. The positive effect of this experience remained with me throughout the day. It was hard for me not to recall the beginning of my career and the discouraging words of the oral surgeon. How I had believed these words for so long!

One of the biggest sins is to leave this world with your music still in you. Only by being your best will you find happiness. Even as I lay in bed that night, I contemplated this. Then I started to think about all the other times someone else's opinion (or my own) had affected what I thought to be true. How I believed I could never afford to attend all the continuums at the Pankey Institute. How I thought restorative dentistry could not be done in a small town, or how the fear of public speaking would keep me away from any lecturing experiences. It wasn't until I was almost asleep that I realized something more important had happened. When I first started my practice, I had a goal to have a position where I could diagnose patient problems and formulate a treatment plan. After I had performed these procedures, another doctor would complete the treatment for the patient. I loved the challenge of solving the problem; I wrote this down as a nonspecific goal. When I told my parents, they were concerned.

"How could you possibly do that?"

I didn't know. My initial vision was that I would be involved in a teaching program in a general practice residency, but this never worked out the way I had envisioned. But after that surgery in my friend's office, I realized my goal had come true with a select group of restorative dentists with whom I am blessed to work. I would help with the diagnosis and work out a treatment plan. The treatment plan was so specific that in the edentulous areas, I would point to where the new teeth would be directed by the implants I placed. Then the patient was returned to the doctor to complete the necessary treatment.

Goals are powerful! They should be written, specific, and in great detail. The more specific your goals, the more predictable your result. Goals are like the target at which you take aim. They are the magnets that pull you through the hard times. As you proceed along the way, you will be hurt; you will find disappointment and failure. But it is your goals that will pull you through these difficult times. They will also pull you through the negative opinions of other people. *You can hit the bull's-eye.* Just make your move before you are ready. Leap, and the net will appear. Always heed the warnings of life and follow the examples of people who are accomplishing what you want. Dream, and your dream will come true.

After the goals have been laid out, a timetable for completion must be created. Each step necessary to accomplish the major goals must be spelled out with an associated time frame. Without a time deadline, there is no way we can stay on track. It is the deadline we impose on ourselves that compresses our thinking and enables us to complete much more than we could normally do.

Experts Needed:
Will You Apply

I hope the month of February was very enjoyable for you, culminating with our annual midwinter meeting in Chicago! It is always a great opportunity to gather new information, get together with old friends, and take a break from the day-to-day schedule! The finest course I attended was an Exquisite Dentures event presented by Dr. Joe Massad. I have been wanting to upgrade my denture technique for awhile, and this was a great opportunity for me. I was not disappointed by this most recent Gordon Christenson Award winner!

Dr. Massad was a senior at Loyola Dental School in Chicago when I was a freshman there. Additionally, we had taken several week-long courses together at the Pankey Institute. In 1987, we took the removable prosthetic course together, and it covered essentially the same information that he is now presenting in 2006. The key to his success was that he had improved the technique so that it was more understandable, and also provided a support group of people to allow each dentist to successfully accomplish this technique.

After attending this class, I was left with some questions: Why was it that Joe decided to become an expert in the denture procedure? Why do some dentists work so diligently on their provisionals that it makes it difficult for the laboratory to achieve the same result? Why do some doctors spend large amounts of time perfecting their preparations and doing their own exquisite gold-inlay lab work? Why do some doctors become great teachers and others great writers?

I believe the answers are simple. These doctors find something they love to do and determine the best ways to become experts in their fields. It has been said that one hour of study each night for five years will make you a world expert on that subject. Why not find these opportunities in our work and become the experts to our patients? I have seen people follow this plan and become the most spiritually, emotionally, and economically rewarded individuals. I wish you the same success!

Can You Hear Me Now?

There is a unique national park in the eastern United States. It is called the Appalachian Trail. This is a hiking trail that starts in the northern part of Georgia and continues through the mountains, spanning Tennessee, North and South Carolina, West Virginia, Virginia, Pennsylvania, New York, New Hampshire, and Vermont, and ends about 2,200 miles later in the northern part of Maine. Along the trail, there are little areas for camping, and small, open huts in strategic locations to shield hikers from the elements.

Some people will hike certain segments of the trail; others will do the entire trail in two-week sections over several years. Finally, there is a hardy group that will start in early spring on the southern end and hike continuously until they finish in the fall in Maine. These hikers are call thru-hikers, and several will finish the entire trail. A very fast and continuously paced hiker would complete it all in four months.

When we were driving through Massachusetts on I-90 on a family vacation, I looked up to see that the bridge we were passing under was labeled the Appalachian Trail. I was surprised, because usually when I am on a trip I look on the map to see where the Appalachian Trail is and see what the country looks like at that point in the trail. This time, I was not aware that we would be intersecting it during our travels. As we passed under the bridge, we could see a hiker passing over the highway. My family told me he had a long, scraggly beard. Was this one of the thru-hikers who had started in late April in Georgia and was now in Massachusetts? He would be over half done, but would still have a lot of hiking and a lot of mountains to climb. I wonder what would be going through his mind at that point. The excitement of starting the hike had certainly passed. He proved that you could do it, and get used to not having the comforts that we all take for granted. The scenery was great, but it wasn't much different from Virginia or Tennessee. I have been told that at this point in the hike, the majority of thoughts during the day revolve around what the hikers are going to eat next. Terrible hunger sets in from the extreme amount of calories burnt by all the hiking and mountain climbing. This particular hiker might have had close to two months of hiking to go. This kind of situation can erode any person's resolve on a long-term goal.

Whenever you set a long-term goal for yourself, it is always suggested to visualize what is going to happen as you finish the goal. How are you going to feel? What are people going to say? In the case of the hiker, what will his extreme physical condition be when he finishes? Visualizing the finish will allow us to look over the sometimes dreary and monotonous middle. It is the same for us—when we blaze the trail for our practice and our patients, we must keep our eyes on the prize!

Our Home Sweet Home

Over the past several years, I have served as an officer of the American Board of General Dentistry. In this time, I have had the opportunity to meet with dentists from other countries, and also military dentists who may move as many as ten times during their careers. These moves may take them to foreign countries for extended stays.

Every person, including those born in another country, tells me that we, as United States citizens, do not know how lucky we are to be living in this country. Business is easier and much more profitable in this country. Not only that, but, as bad as we think our politicians are, other countries' politicians are much worse. In fact, a big payoff to politicians is considered a way of life. Everything costs much more because of the duty that must be paid to those in charge.

We are so blessed to be here. We know this fact, but sometimes we take it for granted. Why else would so many people from other countries be struggling to move here? Certainly, taxes are high, but if that is the cost to keep this enterprise system going, it is a bargain. When I look back at the higher tax rates of the seventies, this seems like nothing.

Opportunities are surrounding us. Make a concentrated effort this week to look for one new source of business. One new client each week can make a considerable difference in your prosperity level by the end of the year. We must take advantage of every opportunity we are offered here, in our wonderful country!

Benchmarking

Once you have your goals are set, written, and defined, it is important to make sure you are carrying through with the implementation of what you have decided to do. If part of your plan involves making contacts to create business, start documenting how many you do in a day, week, and month. The moment you start measuring, your completion rate is going to improve if for no other reason than you are looking at it. Next, if you are motivated to complete your goal on time, or ahead of schedule, you will start to increase the numbers. This discipline needs to be maintained in all parts of your life to make sure that you are staying on track and moving in the direction you wish.

Do What You Love

Because so much of our time is devoted to our work, it is very important that we love what we do. Certainly there are times when we have to do something we can't stand doing, but we must ensure that it is for a short time, or that it is directly leading us to what we desire. With every prize, there is a price to be paid. The price may be money, time, research, study, or doing some difficult discipline that will lead you to what you desire. Part of this process may be uncomfortable, but it is through this discipline that you will be led down the right path.

At one time in my life, I wanted to teach some of the techniques I was learning. I first had to learn to photograph what I did. Next, I had to learn how to create a story with the pictures of the techniques I was performing. These photographs were projected onto large screens, so the photographic techniques needed to be perfect because the photos were going to be magnified. All of this required study and practice to become the person I wished to portray with my presentation. It took a lot of work to get this all together, but it was nothing compared the mountain I still had to climb—I was afraid to get in front of people and talk. Big problem if you want to teach in front of a large audience. I first started out with a Dale Carnegie course on public speaking. Every time I would go to the class, I would dread it. I was continually worried about what they were going to make us do. Well, I have to admit that I did survive. I improved so much I was asked several times to be a teaching assistant for other courses. Later, I took a course titled Strategic Presentations. We learned how to best use our multimedia resources to get our point across to the audience members. Later, we would give presentations, which were videotaped. These were critiqued, and then we would have to give the presentation again with the noted suggestions. Today, I get an immense feeling of power every time I give a presentation, for it represents an expression of me overcoming my fear and ultimately achieving my goal.

What was the important component which was attached to me signing up for the first Dale Carnegie Course in public speaking? Right! I was stepping out of my comfort zone. It is easy for all of us to get on a path that is very comfortable, and it really does not take a lot of effort to stay there. Other paths may appear to lead to riches, but the unknown is a possible risk. It is uncomfortable to try something new. To start a new program can be embarrassing. It's difficult to present an ungraceful appearance or, even worse, the possibility of a public expression of failure. When we start to identify things that are important to us, we see that some of the steps might be uncomfortable. They will cause us to stretch and push and move to places where we have not gone before. The only way to advance is to move into this area. It would be helpful to find someone who has done this same thing before and has overcome the same fears. So, if you have a fear of public speaking, someone like me could help you, since I have felt the same panic and dread prior to my presentations. This could be just enough to push you into action. I know that if you stay in your comfort zone, change or improvement will not be in your future. I want you to have more than the standard fare for your supper— step up to the banquet of a lifetime!

A Ship in a Harbor Is Safe, but That Is Not What Ships Are Built For

Two summers ago, I tried something new. I launched my small, sixteen-foot boat on Trail Creek in Michigan City and went out onto Lake Michigan for the first time. I want to tell you that it was a nervous experience, for I had heard stories about the big lake. I always had respect for the lake. Looking out from the beach on a very clear day, I could make out the buildings in downtown Chicago. When we went out in the boat, all we saw was water all around us, and it was very unsettling. The lake is like a huge desert; it all looks the same. My son and I would go out and try to fish, but there were always problems. First, the anchor I had was not strong enough to hold the boat in the waves. When I got that settled, I got a tip that the perch were biting half a mile off Mount Baldy. That was great news, but our perception of distance was not good. We were fishing probably two miles out instead of half a mile. It took awhile to figure out that mistake. And by the time we got to the location, the fish were full!

One summer went by, and things made more sense. We could find the fish, and we could find our way around, too. We knew the difference between rollers and breakers. We knew that the doughnut was not something to eat, but a place to fish. The rock pile, the lighthouse, and the blue water tower were all familiar landmarks by then. We knew where the black ditch and Burn's Ditch were located. We even knew which one had water flowing in it and which one didn't. Our boat was temporarily on the spot out on the lake where the states of Michigan, Indiana, and Illinois come together. We knew the place where you could be in Indiana in the water and Illinois on the shore.

We were witness to the Tri-State Regatta participants tied up to one another on Trail Creek close to the Old Lighthouse. As the sails went up, it was like a kaleidoscope of colors. Then, one by one, the sailboats would let their lines loose of each other and head for Chicago, which was not visible to those of us in Michigan City that day. Anyone, regardless of navigational training, could have found Chicago that day simply by following the line of boats. Anyone flying into Chicago that day experienced quite a spectacular view of the regatta!

Now, when we attend boat shows, we wonder who will buy the fifty-foot yachts on display. After taking a trip to Chicago and back in our larger thirty-foot boat and knowing what the gas for that trip cost, we wonder if that new yacht owner will keep the ship in its slip. We have neighbors in the marina who rarely take their boat out and are always asking us about the water. They want us to talk about the day the lake was so calm, and in the next hour, the waves were so big that when we went over them, we could hear the propellers come out of the water.

None of these experiences or adventures would be possible had we not overcome out initial nervousness. What are we nervous about in our dental practices? Are we afraid to present the very best treatment plan for fear of rejection? It's time to present those treatment plans and to let our patients decide—the outcome will amaze you! If I can help you with your treatment plans in any way, please do not hesitate to call.

Hurricane Andrew

During a well-planned family vacation at Disney World last year, my mind drifted back to a not-so-well-planned trip to Orlando six years ago …

The night before the trip, we had friends over to the house, so we did not watch the news and did not hear about the preparations being made in Florida for an incoming hurricane. I boarded the plane for Miami with no idea I was headed for difficulty. In my mind, I was simply on my way to be a teaching assistant for a class of Japanese dentists at the Pankey Institute.

As I settled into my seat for the three-hour flight, the captain announced that Hurricane Andrew had just been upgraded to a class-four hurricane and was headed directly for Miami. How bad could this be? The hurricane had the same name we had picked for one of our future children. If I had known my son, Andrew, at this time, I would have worried. Actually, I had been in Florida several times as a youth. When hurricanes had come around, nothing much ever happened—just lots of wind and rain. In my mind, class four wasn't bad; I thought they probably went to class twenty. I drifted off to sleep instead of making plans for what to do when we landed.

Waiting in the luggage return area, I started to worry. There must have been two full news crews from Chicago, arriving with their complete equipment. It was then I learned that few hurricanes were more powerful than the one due to hit Miami in twelve hours. I had not made plans to rent a car. I had expected to stay on Key Biscayne. I had clothes for more than a week, golf clubs, and two carriers full of ten-slide carousels. I planned to help teach C4, and then stay over for a faculty enhancement workshop. In my spare time, I was going to work on a seminar I would give later that year. I must have looked as if I were about to travel the world.

I had to make some quick decisions. First, I had to secure transportation. Announcements in the airport indicated that the last few flights would leave in the next hour. Remaining airplanes would be flown to a safe location and the airport closed. *In life, we can go without goals and preparation, and we will be carried along by every current. Once we realize we are off course, well-defined goals will put us right back on track.*

The car rental desks were closing, and their staff members were directing people to go to the offices that were off the airport grounds. I did not want to leave the airport without a rental car. Finally, I found a desk that was open with a fairly long line. It inched forward. The attendant announced not everyone would be served there and directed us to go to a facility off the airport property. Then, I heard an announcement that I had an urgent message. *In life there are influences that try to take us off our intended paths. If our goals are deeply imprinted on our subconscious minds, we will make the right decisions when necessary.*

I stood in line and got a reservation before the desk closed. I may never know who was paging me in the airport. When I arrived at the parking lot, there were only three cars left. As I loaded luggage into my assigned car, I realized there were about fifty people in the rental office attempting to get cars. I may have rented the very last car available that day.

Next, I called my wife, Nancy, who had heard about the hurricane and was worried about my safety and well-being. She knew the C4 instructor and class had already left for Orlando, but she didn't know their current location. I drove north on the turnpike, heading for Orlando.

As I drove north, Nancy used the phone to find a place for me to stay that night, and to find the C4 destination. As I traveled, the traffic thickened. Before I was out of the Miami area, traffic was at a crawl. Three lanes had become five, with cars driving on the median and shoulder. Two and a half hours later, I was out of the Miami area. *Many times we will be following everyone else and not be aware of the opportunities present.*

As I approached an overpass, I could see people on the bridge. They were motioning to the right. Occasionally, a car would turn off into the grass, drive through an open gate, and onto a dirt road. I looked at the people on the bridge, the dirt road, and the hundreds of miles of traffic. I turned right. No one followed me. Doubt started to creep into my mind. The dirt road turned sharply to the left and took me to the road where the people were standing on the bridge. To the right was the entrance ramp for I-95, a northbound highway that runs along the coast. The traffic was relatively light. *Sometimes the way to get there is not the most direct route. We need to*

*be open to changes and take advice from
people who are likely to know.*

My traveling went smoothly then, but
my wife was not having a good time.
Apparently, travel to the area had been
particularly slow that week, and most hotels
had less than optimal numbers of staff. They
were not prepared to take on this mass
relocation. After making about forty calls, she
did find me a room at an Orlando Airport
hotel. When I got there to check in, the people
there looked at me as if I were insane. They
were completely booked. The reservation my
wife had made had been logged for the
following month. *In case presentation and
sales, never take no as the definite answer. It
is a known fact that the majority of sales
happen after at least seven attempts to close.
If you present one time only and take no as
the answer, you are missing out on a fortune.
And, unfortunately, your patient is missing
out on your fine care.*

When I called Nancy to tell her I was
going to sleep in the car, she told me to go
back to the hotel where the reservation
mistake was made. She had used all the
emotion and persuasion a pregnant woman
could muster to convince the manager to let
me sleep on a rollaway bed in one of the

ballrooms. When I arrived at the hotel, the manager shook my hand, assigned me a room on the concierge level of the hotel, and then I snacked on appetizers before going to bed eighteen hours after I left home. I wondered if Mary and Joseph would have been turned away if Nancy had been along …

The next morning, as Hurricane Andrew roared through Key Biscayne, denuding and damaging much of the island, hardly a raindrop fell on Orlando. Later in the day, I joined the C4 class, and we made the absolute best of the situation. In true Pankey Institute style, fine lectures and discussions were held, and special Orlando-style entertainment enjoyed. The Japanese had both a quality learning experience and a memorable visit to Florida.

Certainly, you would think this was a once-in-a-lifetime experience. So would I, except I was the teaching assistant two years later when The Pankey Institute had to evacuate for the second time in its history for another hurricane. But that's another story.

Information Overload—
This Server Is Full!

Yesterday I was going through my e-mail. Every day I get updates from several organizations I am involved with. I get newsletters and reports. Doctors will occasionally send me radiographs to prepare for a pre-consultation appointment. Friends send me short notes, and finally, I do receive spam. All sorts of advertisements from continuing education to drugs appear in my mail. The messages are relentless. I have noticed that my e-mail folder fills up by the hour. I was looking at my e-mail system, which I have had for only two years, and I have already deleted ten thousand messages. The average daily amount is going up each month. I think this number is an average amount for a business account. My spam amount is characteristic of anyone who uses the Internet to conduct business.

A frequent topic of conversation is the overload of information each of us must deal with each day. It is becoming increasingly difficult for us to break through this information avalanche to get our messages across. The only way that we can make an impact is to break our message into two parts. First of all, we must differentiate ourselves; second, we must include some sort of emotional trigger within our message. Something must touch the person in a way that they will choose the correct course. To be effective in this process, we need to know the person well enough to find out what is motivating for them. Emotional content is what makes us want to do something. The facts are merely there is help us justify our decision.

A Mentor:
the Ultimate Time-Saver

Jim Rohn would say to work harder on yourself than you work on your job! If you work hard on your job, you will make a living. If you work hard on yourself, you will make a fortune. The discipline to continue to work on yourself and to keep yourself focused will allow you to create rewarding opportunities.

We need to focus energy on ourselves—to improve, to be more effective. It is out of this mentality that we feel better about ourselves. We have to have a constant input of good material into our brains to sustain us. We need self-improvement books in every discipline important to us. They can be books on motivation, spiritual enlightenment, management, delegation, and the list goes on and on. Can the farmer expect to harvest a crop without first planting the seed? Just like the farmer, we have to work on improving ourselves so that we deserve to have good results, and to also know how to handle those successes appropriately.

Sometimes it feels like we are not making progress as fast as we would like. This is usually the time when a decision needs to be made. Do you want to spend time, which we only have a limited amount of, to investigate all the different ways to accomplish our goals? Many times with this approach we will reach several dead ends, or simply be doing the wrongs things for awhile until we realize our mistake. One way to avoid this is to find someone who is doing what we want and follow what they are doing to allow us to get the same result. We are, in essence, trading our money to buy a certain amount of experience. We are also allowing ourselves to sidestep disappointment and wasted time when we make this choice. Unfortunately, we cannot just hire a coach and then expect our success to be around the corner. There is a need to implement what is learned. In the movies *Miracle* and *Hoosiers*, the coaches truly believe their teams will win despite staggering odds. Both coaches put the teams through endless drills and workouts to increase their skills and physical conditioning. In both of these situations, who maps out the plays? Who develops the program? The coach. Who does the endless sprints, the sit-ups, and endlessly works on the plays through drills so that they work seamlessly without thought? The players. Does everyone know how to run the plays immediately after the coach has shown them to the team? No! The team has to work on them. The faster the implementation, the quicker the result, and the less likely the necessary work will be put aside and not done. One of the greatest rules of success is to do things fast. The moment you realize you want to do something, you need to start on it. Much of the work that keeps us busy during the day is not productive. Once we find the thing that will guarantee us success, everything not immediately associated with our success should be put on hold. We must focus on the final outcome!

Who Needs a Coach?

You know professional athletes do. Actors
do. Singers do. Salespeople do. Nearly every
professional does. Why do we as
professionals spend so much on education
and technology, but then do not invest in
coaching to help us to reach our potential? It
is a fact that dentistry is usually practiced at a
level below what is accepted to be the
standard of our profession. The reason is that
our patients do not accept our
recommendations for comprehensive care. It
is my belief that is because we have had no
formal training in giving sales presentations.
It is not difficult to convince people they need
a filling or an extraction of a fractured tooth.
But when it comes to leading a person to the
decision that he or she needs an upper and
lower quadrant of crowns to correct the plane
of occlusion, difficulty sets in. There is
increased cost to the patient, and insurance
does not effectively cover treatment like this.
These facts put us on the same playing field
with a salesperson presenting a fee for an
investment like life insurance.

The most effective way to check on your presentation skills is to videotape yourself in action. Videotape it, and then let a dentist you trust look at it with you. Better yet, have a salesperson look at it—possibly someone in a field not related to dentistry, and see what he thinks. I know that if a golf professional got into a slump, the video camera would help to identify his problem. Our presentations might be too technical, or they may not include the emotional viewpoint and then use the technical information to justify the purchase.

Some of the best time and money I ever spent was during my affiliation with the Dale Carnegie course on public speaking. The course gave me the chance to work on expressing ideas in a clear fashion. I liked the course so much that I became a teaching assistant for several years. Finally, I took a course given by their organization called Strategic Presentations. Among the members of the group were CEOs of large corporations who needed to give important sales and promotional presentations. We all were required to give five presentations to the group. Each one was videotaped, and we were given critiques on our performances and how we could improve our next presentation.

Who needs a coach? We all do, at different times. You might need a coach for technical, presentational, organizational, or promotional reasons. I say write this as I'm signing myself up for another year of coaching. I hope my coach has a good coach!

Take Your Best Shot!

Several years ago, my son, Andrew, and I were camping with his Cub Scout pack. During the day, there were a number of activities to keep the boys busy. The boys were very excited about the possibility of shooting a rifle. When we got to that section, darkness started to set in, and the area was thick with mosquitoes. The shooting glasses started to fog up, and Andrew didn't do too well with his shooting.

The next year at camp, however, the conditions were perfect for shooting. I couldn't believe it, but Andrew was struggling to even hit the target. Everything about his form seemed correct to me, but the target was elusive. The director of the activity came over, and we explained Andrew's problem. He had Andrew look at him, and he did a few exercises, and the director said he discovered his problem. We already knew our son was ambidextrous. When he started school, he would write with one hand and then use the other hand the next time. Finally, he chose his right hand as dominant. The strange thing we found out that day was that he was left-eye dominant. When he lined up as a right-handed marksman, the wrong eye was lined up with the sight, and he could not hit the target. By moving his head slightly over, his left eye was aligned with the sight, and then every shot hit the bull's-eye.

We can see this story illustrated in our practices. We can have everything (and I mean *everything*) set up the way we think it should be, and not enjoy the success we desire. We then have several options: give up, redesign everything, and try an entirely different approach, or look for one or two different things that, if discovered, can spell success. Look for the person who is successful in your field and see what they are doing. Read a book. Go to a seminar. But don't give up! Giving up sends you back to the starting line again. Chances are that you are one good idea away from the success you want!

Our Book Club Meetings

Trying to make a connection with children is sometimes difficult. It is hard for me to relate to what the kids today are going through. Of course, the world was different for me as a child all those years ago. I can remember what it was like, but it has hardly any similarities with what my kids are going through today. We had no cell phones, no computers. The grade school I went to had two grades in each class. So in first grade, my class was on one side of the room, and the second grade was on the other side. Somehow the teacher would alternate from one class to the next. I walked to school every day until I was a sophomore in high school.

It was a really big deal when an astronaut orbited the earth and was found alive when the capsule was recovered in the ocean. Cars had no seat belts, and in coupes the backseat seat did not lock, so if the car stopped fast you could very easily end up in the front seat. People wrote letters a lot, and actually talked on the telephone instead of texting. When we called my grandmother in Chicago, which was fifty miles away, you first had to call the operator for her to make the connection. It is challenging to make a connection with today's kids because the world is so much different now that it was when I was young.

What my wife, Nancy, and I did was to follow some very good advice as our kids were growing up. It was recommended that we read them five hundred books by the time they started any type of school. Of course, somewhere before we reached the five hundredth book, both of our children were starting to understand the written text. So as they got older, that would be one of our meeting places, the point where we could have the same experience. As they grew, I can remember going to get a new printing of a series of books. I would not be able to get just one; I would have to get one for each member of the family, and then we would race to see who would finish first. From this place, we could have a conversation about a shared experience. It was also a starting point for discussions about how what we had learned affected us. From this point, we could share other thoughts and conversations.

As they became tweens, it was their music. We listened to their music and knew the artists they admired. Once I was watching a show on Sunday morning about one of the stars who had just had a string of number-one hits. When she auditioned for *American Idol*, she was cut immediately. But with persistence, combined with family support, she was finally able to be recorded and get her music played. What a wonderful story to discuss with a teenager! Once there is a common point of interest, new conversations and information can be shared. Ultimately, a new depth of relationship can be obtained.

This technique is also helpful in business. It is integral to our business success to make emotional and personal connections with others. Certainly, if you would like to partner with someone and help her to achieve her goals, you must work to find a common thread to find out what is important to her and how you may be of service to her.

The Art of Saying No

Once you are known to be proficient in completing projects, people will be asking you to help them with theirs. This may be a charity event or help with a project at church, or you may be asked to be involved in some sort of business venture. If you are not careful, you will be involved with a project you really had no intention of working on, or overbooked with work so that you cannot put your energies into the projects that need to be accomplished. It is flattering for someone to come up to you and want you to be involved with them.

The tendency is to automatically say yes to a project. Once you have said yes, it is nearly impossible to get out of it without a misunderstanding. It is better to indicate that you are very involved in several projects at the time. Could you get an estimate of the amount of involvement? Are meetings necessary? Everyone knows that meetings will dramatically increase your time commitment in nearly everything. Can you work on the project by yourself, and just give e-mail updates? Try your best to get an accurate estimate of the time commitment. Try this: "I am flattered to be asked to be involved in this project, but I need to check my prior time commitments. I would hate to take on something new that could not receive my full attention. I will be back in touch with you tomorrow." Then it is time to look at the schedule of projects you are currently involved with. Check to see how this project fits into the master plan of your goals and how this new addition will mesh with the rest. Check at home to see how this might affect your domestic activities. Now that the pressure is off, you can look at this intelligently and give an answer the next day. If you do say yes, you may have to impose conditions. The more successful you become, the more you will have to work on the art of saying no.

Commands for Your Success

This section is my memory of a presentation that I witnessed over twenty-five years ago. The day had such an impact on me that I duplicated a card given to me that day. The presentation was given by Dr. L. D. Pankey and Dr. Harold Wirth. Dr. Pankey spent the morning reviewing his philosophy of dental practice, and the way he had developed his practice. Dr. Wirth spent the afternoon essentially building up our mental images of ourselves, making us truly believe that if we could conceive and believe in our dreams, we could achieve them. The final session of the day was spent with Dr. Wirth, reviewing this card. Dr. Wirth told us the cards were sized so we could keep them in our wallets with our money, so we could refer to them often. If you feel inclined, you can copy these sides of the card, attach them back to back, and laminate them to keep these thoughts with you. (Copy of this card is found on the last page of the book).

His first command for success was to follow the cross of life, which Dr. Pankey had talked about in his lecture.

As you can see, there are four titles at each end of the cross. Each represents an aspect of our lives that deserves our attention, so that we have balance in our lives. When you find this balance, happiness will be a companion. Working all the while is not enough for the human spirit. In the Bible, there is reference to a day of rest. I do not know if this was intended to be a day of play or a day of worship, but it was certainly not meant to be a day of work. In our society, with all of its technological advances, we are able to accomplish much more in a shorter amount of time. This fast pace can wear on us. We need to heed our instincts and then take some time to regenerate our bodies, spirits, and relationships. These are navigation points for our lives. The amount of work does not have to have to be balanced by an equal amount of play.

Every one of us needs different proportions of these to find balance. If you find that you have neglected a portion of your life, just correct it. If you have neglected relationships you cherish, let the other people know you have realized this deficiency and now plan to pay it back with interest. I personally find that after a busy five-day work week, I am feeling spent. I love my work, and I am blessed to be in a profession where I am continually helping people. I am constantly being rewarded by the appreciation others give to me and my family. The physical and emotional nature of my work, however, leaves me starting to feel spent by the end of the week. My wife tells me that I try to set up the weekend as if I am on vacation. Every weekend I have a full plate of tennis, golf, fishing, boating, or travel to a different area for a short trip. I need the break, and have reconciled that I also deserve it. It also helps me buffer other occurrences happening around me, which I frankly do not have much control over.

Right now, it seems everyone is concerned with the economy and the changes in their stock market portfolios. Recently, our family retirement plan has suffered some setbacks. It seems that if things stay as they are, retirement may be put off for awhile. Is this a big concern to me? Not really. I love my work, and every weekend I have a short vacation, a small piece of what most people look for in retirement. I just do it a little every week. I love my lifestyle, and it is really my intention to keep doing what I love. If, next year, I cut back on one aspect of my work, say the clinical aspect, and replace it with more writing, more teaching, and have extra time for some of my other pursuits, then I see myself balancing my life like this for some time.

I have, in recent times, added at least one two-week vacation a year. This gives me a sample of how retirement would be in the traditional sense of things. I feel myself being rested during the first week. Into the second weekend, the days of play start to be less exciting. At this time, I feel the tug to get back to some sort of work, for I feel the need to have some mental challenges. By the time we get back home, I am ready to be back at my work. Actually, by that time, I am looking forward to it. The other two points are difficult to explain. Not the concept of each, but rather the implementation of each. I know that my relationship with my family is the most important thing to me. If I became famous for my work and received the acclaim of others but lost the love of my family, this would not create a situation I could live with or bear. For this reason, I am constantly looking for ways to be part of their routines and schedules. There have been times in my life when I have not been totally engaged in spending time worshipping God. Fortunately for me, there was a time I started to question my relationship with my religion and the practices of it. I spent a year reading about it, and came out of this study with a new appreciation and understanding of my religion. I know that this aspect may take on a different form for everyone. In fact, you may not even acknowledge a God in your life. If that is the case, I would recommend that you have a small amount of time each week where you can be by yourself. During this quiet time, allow your mind to work and not be interrupted by the pressures and stimulations of the world around us.

The second command is to keep a positive mental attitude.

In many books and philosophical studies, we are reminded that we are what we think about becoming. Marcus Aurelius said, "The world in which we live is determined by our thoughts." Think about good, honest, wholesome things, and that is what you become. Think about corrupt, dishonest, and hurtful things, and that is the way you will act. Think positive thoughts, and positive things will continuously arrive in your life. The mind tunes into these thoughts, and they become a type of magnet for positive things. Because you are looking for the positive in the world, those things become evident. When we feel great about ourselves, we can act upon these opportunities.

Negatives precipitate doubt and failures. In my own life, I know that this is absolutely true. The example that comes to mind right now is my tennis game. When I start thinking about the game and the missed shots, my game disintegrates. It is only when the game is fun and I pay attention to the play aspect that I am at my best. Think about the tightrope, and you will fall. Think about an error or a mistake, and you will be drawn to another. Watch a figure skating competition—when one of the skaters falls during her routine, it seems like the performers who follow have an increased chance of the same fate. The fall is on everyone's mind, and so instead of thinking about perfecting the artistic presentation of their routines, the thought of not falling leads them to do just that.

The way we perceive things is modified by our thoughts. Two people will have an entirely different perception of what is happening and of what opportunities are available. As a consequence of my work, there are certain frequencies of sound I do not hear especially well. With other frequencies of sound, I have exceptional hearing. I can be in a room full of people talking, and I can hear a cell phone vibrate across the room when no one else in the room is aware of that sound. A positive mental attitude has the same effect. It can eliminate the buzz of negative thoughts and allow you to be aware of the true opportunities around you.

Socrates tells us, "Know thyself." His philosophy revolved around the examined life. Look at the things we want and the things we don't want. Draw our attention to our wants. Evaluate what we have accomplished in the past year, make note of them, and make it our goal to repeat the things that have worked. Processes that have not worked need to be modified or eliminated. This effort of examining ourselves will keep us out of the rut of life. Former Bulls coach Phil Jackson stated that the "repetition of a flawed technique yields the same result," and it is so true—in basketball and in life.

The third command is to apply goal gradient psychology.

The first important part of this command is the goal. Without goals, we are afloat in a boat on the lake, with no known destination. We are pushed by the wind and current, and we get the impression that we are on our journey. It is a journey, but to where? It could be a journey going to where we do not want to go, doing what we do not want to do, and finally becoming who we do not want to become. If you do not have well-defined goals for yourself, most certainly you will be part of the achievement of someone else's goals. Having our goals outlined for our specific destination helps us to set the sail so that we arrive at the destination we wish. These destinations, of course, are our goals, and the more precisely we have them defined, the more direct our travels will be.

We need to aim high when we are setting goals. A four-minute mile and a trip to the moon were once thought impossible. We are put on this earth by a loving God who only wants the best for us. We have to deliberately think about the best happening to us and expect that it is going to happen. Set your goals in a fashion that will ensure your success. You have to create goals that allow time for you to develop. You cannot go from bad to the best in one step. Many steps have to be taken to get you to your destination. The baby cannot start walking on the first day. The baby has to learn to roll, sit up, crawl, stand, and then finally walk. Yes, there can be some falling involved in this process. If you do fall, get up, brush yourself off, and try it again and again.

The fourth command is to develop the will to do or to be.

Essentially, this is our internal proclamation to the universe that we are going to do something or be something—no matter what. No matter how difficult the going becomes, we will continue to look for ways to arrive at our important goals. The baby who keeps falling on his journey to walking is not told to give up, since he has tried enough. No; the baby is told to keep trying until he walks. This has to be our way of thinking about our goals. We have to keep trying. We must learn and grow from our mistakes and seek out others who can help us. People who have accomplished their goals are always ready to share their journeys with others. Before you ask, do your own homework, and come to the meeting prepared to do what is suggested. Many times, fellow professionals have asked me to be their mentor and to help them achieve success. I find out what they want to accomplish. I make suggestions on their course of study so that they can accomplish tasks and meet goals leading them to their ideal situations.

When I give friends directions to success and explain the associated work and study that is involved, many do not take the first step to help themselves. I know this because so many have not come back to review what they have learned and to proceed to the next step. To become something or do something is not difficult, but it does have a price. The price may be study, practice, or making a financial commitment, and then continually following through with your plan. Dr. Pankey would say, "Oh discontented man—step up, pay the price, and then take it." *It* is what you desire. *It* will never be handed over to you. *It* has to be paid for. The only way to possess *it* is to earn *it*!

In the fifth command, we are told to increase our energy and enthusiasm to enhance our lives.

This seems like an impossible task in this world of ours, where everything and everyone seems to want to take energy away from us. The only healthy way to increase our energy and zest for life is to exercise both physically and mentally. Dr. Wirth advised that we should learn to eat to live and not live to eat. We all know so much about diet and energy and health, it would be such a sin to ignore it. Exercise is a very important component in our health formula. Just a half an hour of walking every other day will reap tremendous health advantages. Can we not donate a half hour to our own health bank to receive amazing returns?

Our minds are exercised by learning and all forms of education, including our attention to good books, tapes, and lectures. We need to exercise our brains in a fashion that gets us up and going each day. Dr. Wirth had a ritual to mentally prepare himself for each new day. He would visualize himself as a warrior returning from a distant land as performed in the opera *Aida*. He would visualize the parade of horses, elephants, and camels. He would see the people lining the streets, paying homage to him on his return as the savior of the teeth of New Orleans. This exercise in particular reminded him of how important he was in his patients' lives. This is one example of Dr. Wirth's mental gymnastics. He would use this small exercise to help him stay grounded in what was important, and why he should be ever grateful for what he could accomplish for his patients. This form of mental gymnastics was perfect for him and his situation, but it might not be appropriate for you.

Personally, I like to have a folder full of cards and letters from patients who have written down words to express their appreciation to me. From time to time, I will pick up this folder and reread the messages. This provides me with the strength to happily get through some of the tougher times in my practice.

Dr. Wirth was ever mindful of how good he had it in his profession. Every time he would see someone doing a job that he found to be less than desirable, he would be thankful he did not have to do that task to earn a living. I live in the Midwest. Our winters can be very cold. One day it was below zero. The water line across the street from my office broke. The men from the water department had to dig a hole to find the leak. Next, they had to get down into the pipe, which was partially filled with water, to fit the new pipe in that freezing weather. Looking out the window of my office, which was at a constant seventy-two degrees, I

said, "I am glad I am not one of those guys."
(Now, it could very well be that one of the
repairmen was looking at my office, saying
he was glad he did not have to work in
someone else's mouth, too.)

Command number six concerns giving of ourselves.

Learn the art of giving freely of yourself.
We can choose to be emotionally available
for our customers and staff. Listening to
others with the intent to solve both emotional
and logical concerns for everyone affected is
most effective. In the professional arena, we
need to be available to create successful
people around us. Many times, in giving of
ourselves, we will find solutions to our
concerns, which we may have thought were
unsolvable. In this success-minded society,
we have to find ways to help others reach
their goals. We need to find ways to be the
person cheering at the finish line for someone
who has just accomplished a personal success
story.

We may think of our personal energy
as a set quantity, so that if we give out
energy, we will have less left. In truth, our
energy   is   refillable,   recyclable,   and

renewable. The replaced energy is of a higher quantity and quality. If we only spill out a little of this energy, then only a little will be replaced. The source of the other person's energy is immense. Actually, we cannot get rid of the energy faster than it can be replaced. The energy will continue to flow into our reserves. Our reserves will be filled so quickly, the energy will be spilling over the sides.

In sharing our expertise with others, we have to be careful how we allocate our time. There are people who will take our suggestions, implement them, and take the meaning of success to a whole new level. Most likely, these will be the people who have been working on their problems and are just stuck right now. They will ask for help and be willing to do whatever it takes to reach their goals.

Other people will be in a situation where if they just did a little, they would improve so much. Unfortunately, these are the people who are convinced that it is hopeless, too hard, or that the advice would not work for their particular problem. One person will be an energy multiplier for you, the other an endless drain.

Command number seven instructs us to become constant students.

We need to continuously find ways to improve the quality and quantity of the service we provide. No one should have to tell you that you need to be a constant student. Our access to new information and knowledge is increasing so quickly that sometimes the temptation is to just give up.

The better choice is to consistently and steadily decrease the scope of focus in our endeavors. By doing this, not only can we keep up with all of the changes, but we are also acting to specialize in our purpose. The more focused we are in our endeavors, the more valuable are our services. I think back to the times when we did not have the solutions to problems that we have today. Doctors would have to sit at meetings and brainstorm for possible solutions to what they saw clinically. They had to develop new techniques to treat what they understood to be problems. We now have the view presented from atop their shoulders, and we need to take advantage of their work as we complete our own.

Command number eight advises us to be humble and to radiate happiness, good cheer, and health.

No one wants to deal with someone who does not appear to feel well. Just as our positive mental attitude is expressed to others, so are our health and happiness. Try to imagine the person you want to work with, have fun with, or have a relationship with, and then strive to be that person. If your goal is to become a successful professional, how would that person look? How would that person talk? What type of friends would that person have? If you define who you want to be in these terms, and strive to fulfill them, you will become that person. In all our successes, we must remain humble. There is nothing worse than being trapped with a bore, at a party or anywhere else. People run from a bore and avoid him at all costs. People want to be around individuals who are interested in their ideas, needs, and goals. We must work to be that person, too.

Command number nine reminds us to help others to their successes.

Indeed, it has to remain top of mind that we help others through their issues in life and business. It is through this teaching process that we personally learn more about ourselves and what we do on a daily basis. Through the justification of what we do to others, we have the opportunity not only to teach and help, but also to solidify to ourselves the processes that we go through. It is essential not only to be at the finish line to congratulate someone in equaling what you have done, but also to find ways for others to surpass what you have done. No matter what your profession or business is, I am sure there are people who have lent you their knowledge or technology to make things better for others. What if that person had kept that information to herself? Of course, progress would not have occurred in a timely fashion. Many people would not have had the benefit of this knowledge and improvement. The people they serve would not have been positively affected either. Dr. Wirth would find great comfort knowing that as he shared his ideas in a large lecture setting, he was not only helping the hundreds of doctors in attendance, but also the thousands of patients each of those doctors treated.

Finally, the tenth command tells us to have complete faith in our creator.

Develop and use the power of prayer. Dr. Wirth would talk about the walks he would take in the early morning in New Orleans's Audubon Park before leaving for work. He would walk around the park, with its oak trees filled with Spanish moss hanging down. In the early morning, as the sun would come up on this very special area, he would say he could not help but get a spiritual uplift from being there. He would not want to walk with anyone during this time, for he wanted his immediate world to be quiet. Dr. Wirth wanted it to be quiet so that if God talked to him, he would be able to hear him. He was afraid that if he was talking to someone else, he might not hear God trying to speak to him. Every one of us needs to listen for voices from above, and to act on what we hear. It is also important during this time of quiet to give thanks for everything we have or have achieved, for we are truly blessed to be given this chance in proving ourselves in this life.

Give It Away

Thank you for spending this time with me! It has been an honor to spend this time with you; I hope you found this a great investment of your time. I know I have received a great amount of energy and focus in my life by putting this together for you. I just want to spend a few moments more on the topic of thanks. In our world, I believe we take too much for granted. We may even believe we are entitled to some of the services around us. People who work for the town, for the government, in the restaurants, at the local store—we expect them to provide a great service, for they are ultimately employed by us, right? We live in a world where there is so little expression of appreciation. I have found that the more appreciation I personally express, the more appreciation is returned to me. In my work as a dentist, I make it a point to thank all my patients before they leave. I thank them for being at my office instead of another one. I thank them for their confidence in me. I thank them for paying their bills on time. The list really could go on and on. I am blessed to have the patients that I do.

Throughout the years, they have put up with me going to continuing education events, and then having some of them try out the new procedures. Their generosity and resources have allowed me to be trained to do the work that I totally enjoy doing today. When treatments did not go as expected, patients have understood and allowed me to continue to treat them until the issue corrected itself.

When my patients receive their thanks, it makes them feel great. By giving this away, I get such a warm feeling that I have done something right. So many people are never acknowledged or respected with proper thanks. People will usually think about it for a minute, since they do not know how to respond to my thanks. Invariably, the next response will be a thank-you for the care and consideration of the treatment they received. What a win-win situation!

We need to be sure we thank the servers at our restaurant tables for their service and for taking care of us so well. Give thanks to the people we work with, for their help in achieving our goals. You would not believe the looks on the faces of the people who worked in the government complex when my wife profusely thanked them for their efficient handling of the property tax issue we had. I guess they were used to getting expressions other than gratitude. How about the teachers who help our children navigate through their studies and move on to the next project? Did you know that in many schools, especially at the end of a grading period, the teachers will huddle in the teacher's lounge after school so that crazed parents cannot find them? I wonder how an expression of sincere appreciation would make them feel. Here is a question for you. If you made someone's day, week, or month better by just a few words, how would that make you feel? Really, how much effort would it take to roll down your car window and yell "thanks" to the police officer directing traffic in the middle of winter in northwest Indiana?

I am asking you to consider saying thank you to show appreciation for other people, and to evaluate how it makes you feel. It is a small part of a success formula for attracting good things your way. This feeling and power will be released with a multitude of different ways of transferring a wealth of positive experiences to you.

Something that is very similar and works the same way is making donations to charity—donations made not for show or for recognition, but more important, for a good feeling. Giving money to your church or a deserving organization will certainly help the people directly involved. You might say, "I only have so much; I really cannot afford to give even the smallest amount away." The truth is that if we hang on to our resources like that, limited amounts of riches will be available for us. If we go with the belief that the universe holds an unlimited amount of resources, we will not be held back by the fear that no more riches will come our way. If a glass is full of water, no more can fit into it. If we pour some out, then there is the opportunity to fit more into it. Once this cycle has started, the replacement of donated resources will outpace our capacity to give it away. There are many stories of wealthy businessmen who spent a large amount of their early lives acquiring wealth, and sometimes, because of poor health or another reason, they decided to give all their money away. Huge fortunes were donated, and then, many years later, when you would have thought the businessmen would be out of money, they were found to be far wealthier than when they started to try to give away their wealth. In one of the stories I shared with you earlier, I talked about donating my time to train for a race to raise funds for the

Leukemia Society. Did I run out of time? No, I expressed the feeling that I had more time, and that my business broke records that summer. So remember: as hard as you try to give it away, you will not be successful, for whatever the gift is, it will be returned to you in some other form.

Dr. Leonard F. Anglis, DDS, ABGD, ABID

Dr. Anglis is a recognized expert in the field of implant dentistry and the restoration of mouths and smiles with complicated and serious problems. He is a graduate of Loyola University School of Dentistry. Following dental school, he spent a year at University of Chicago Hospital, studying with the leaders in the fields of medicine and dentistry. Dr. Anglis has been practicing dentistry in Indiana for over thirty years. He has offices in Lowell, Crown Point, and Michigan City, Indiana. He has the privilege of working with over fifty dentists in the area, providing implant surgical treatment for their patients. Dr. Anglis has been awarded diplomate status in the American Academy of General Dentistry. He has served as president of this national organization and recently was awarded the Buddy Boris Memorial Award for his exceptional service to the organization. He has been awarded diplomate status in the American Board of Implant Dentistry as well. Dr. Anglis has been awarded the fellowship, mastership, and finally the ultimate award of Lifelong Learning and Service to Dentistry by the Academy of General Dentistry. He has headed up the state chapter as president of the Academy of General Dentistry. Dr. Anglis has served on several national committees within this organization. Dr. Anglis has a held a test-writing position on the National Board Examination, which every dentist must pass to become licensed in the United States. He has lectured throughout the United States and has written over fifty published articles. Dr. Anglis is a master trainer for dentists who incorporate implant dentistry in their practices. He lives in Crown Point, Indiana with his wife, Nancy, and their two children, Jaclyn and Andrew.

"COMMANDS FOR YOUR SUCCESS"

1. Work - Play - Love - Worship.

2. Keep Positive Mental Attitude (P.M.A.).
   a. "Know thyself" – Socrates.
   b. Negatives precipitate doubt and failures.
   c. "The world in which we live is determined by our thoughts" – Marcus Aurelius.

3. Apply Goal Gradient Psychology.
   a. Aim High!
   b. Expect the best!
   c. Set up goals, consistent with your circumstances, objectives and temperament, and keep them to yourself.
   d. Have a definite plan.
   e. Visualize yourself as being successful in obtaining your goals.

4. Develop your Will "To Do" - "To Be".
   a. "The normal opener of deeper and deeper levels of energy is the will" – William James.

5. Increase Energy and Enthusiasm.
   a. Be temperate in all things.
   b. Exercise regularly, both physically and mentally (Mental Gymnastics).

6. Learn Art of Giving Freely of Yourself.
   a. Be honest and complimentary.
   b. Demonstrate empathy and sympathy.

7. Be a Constant Student.
   a. Improve quality and quantity of service consistent with goal set in command #3.

8. Be Humble - Radiate Happiness, Good Cheer and Health.
   a. Be gentle.
   b. Be a good citizen.

9. Help Others to Their Successes.
   a. Share your knowledge and experiences.

10. Have Complete Faith in Your Creator.
    a. Develop and use the power of prayer.

ELIMINATE NEGATIVE	ACCENTUATE POSITIVE
1. Can't	1. Can
2. Ill	2. Will do
3. Doubt	3. Certainty
4. Worry	4. Think – Be Confident
5. Don't have time	5. Will have time
6. Maybe	6. Positively
7. Fear	7. Courage - Faith
8. Disbelief	8. Internal peace
9. Frustration	9. Tranquility
10. Minimize "I" in conversation.	10. Accentuate "You" - make everyone feel important - compliment!

in loving Memory of

Dr. F. Harold Wirth